C. L. R. James on the 'Negro Question'

C. L. R. James on the 'Negro Question'

By C. L. R. James

Edited and with an introduction by Scott McLemee

University Press of Mississippi
Jackson

Copyright © 1996 by the University Press of Mississippi
Manufactured in the United States of America
99 98 97 96   4 3 2 1
The paper in this book meets the guidelines for permanence and durability of the
Committee on Production Guidelines for Book Longevity of the Council on Library
Resources.

Library of Congress Cataloging-in-Publication Data

James, C. L. R. (Cyril Lionel Robert), 1901-1989
    C.L.R. James on the "Negro question" / by C.L.R. James ; edited and with an
introduction by Scott McLemee.
        p.   cm.
    Includes bibliographical references and index.
    ISBN 0-87805-807-9 (alk. paper). — ISBN 0-87805-823-0 (pbk. : alk. paper)
    1. Afro-Americans—History.   2. Blacks—Caribbean Area—History.
3. United States—Race relations.   I. McLemee, Scott.   II. Title.
E185.J326   1996
973'.0496073—dc20   96-3385
                                                                         CIP

British Library Cataloging-in-Publication data available

Contents

Preface

Between *The Black Jacobins* (1938) and *Beyond a Boundary* (1963), a shadow falls. These books have been established—through an informal yet powerful consensus—as the landmark works of C. L. R. James's career. *The Black Jacobins* recounts "the only successful slave revolt in history," the San Domingo uprising. *Beyond a Boundary* almost defies categorization: it is an autobiographical, sociological, and historical meditation on the fine art of cricket, particularly as that game is played in the West Indies. (It is a book about cricket in much the same way *Moby Dick* is "about" deep-sea fishing.) These are luminous books, artful works of narrative prose, from the pen of an author unusually sensitive to the interaction between historical processes and the historian's craft. Had C. L. R. James written nothing else, these pioneering studies of African-diasporic political and cultural analysis would secure his reputation.

And so: a shadow falls between them. But that image—two masterpieces looming, monument-like, above a darkling plane, with the rest of his work obscured—applies in another sense as well. A quarter century passed between *The Black Jacobins* and *Beyond a Boundary*. During that period C. L. R. James published no sustained work of historical prose. His attention was trained, rather, largely on questions of Marxist politics and theory. James, who could write so movingly about the revolt in Haiti or the nuances of a batsman's style, devoted no less seriousness to arguing against the Three Theses on Retrogressionism of the External Committee of the International Communists of Germany in the mid-1940s. He devoted enormous energy to working out positions in disputes many of which were so obscure that no historian has yet prepared their chronicle.

Little wonder, then, if the period between James's major books has remained, for most readers, terra incognita. A few of his writings from that quarter century have found their enthusiasts. Most, however, are now subject to what Marx once called "the gnawing criticism of the mice." But among James's interim writings there are a number of documents which, once rescued from oblivion, still seem interesting and alive. Such is the case, I think, with the texts collected here: fragments of his effort to work out a Marxist analysis of African-American life.

Published between 1939 and 1950, at the height of James's involvement in the Trotskyist movement, they form a distinct set of writings within the much larger body of his work. The earliest text included here, "Preliminary Notes on the Negro Question," was prepared for Trotsky himself, while the latest pieces were composed as James was writing *American Civilization* and *State Capitalism and World Revolution*, the two works through which, in 1950, he broke entirely with the Russian's ideas.

Yet the deeper coherence of this volume lies not so much in James's political allegiance during those years as in the concentration on black movements for liberation. Those struggles could be interpreted through Marxist concepts. But those struggles develop according to a logic of their own. James's work is driven, then, by a certain tension between Marxist theory and the circumstances of African-American history and experience. There were moments of blindness, and James knew it, but the author of *The Black Jacobins* also brought a distinctive intelligence and sensibility to questions that had concerned American Marxists for years.

In assembling James's writings on "the Negro question," I have tried to produce a book that might be something more than a congeries of scattered pieces. The introduction provides biographical information about the period during which James wrote the material gathered here. Every choice of fact or emphasis is, in itself, a kind of interpretation; and I have attempted to keep explicit commentary and analysis to a bare minimum. But I hope that this set of James's writings—the selection of texts or excerpts and their arrangement here in a particular sequence—will demonstrate that, over the course of a dozen years, he studied the American scene with a trained eye.

One somewhat rigid criterion has governed the selection of items for this book. With one exception, the writings gathered here have never been reprinted before. A number of them are not even listed in the best available bibliographies of James's work; in a few cases, the original publications in which they appeared are now very scarce. I have never reprinted a text simply because it is rare or unusual. But given the choice between reproducing documents available elsewhere and including material that has been neglected, I have taken the latter course.

As noted, there is one exception. By now, "The Revolutionary Answer to the Negro Problem in the United States" (1948) has been rather widely anthologized. James considered it one of the major writings of his American years, and rightly so. "The Revolutionary Answer" marks the culmination of his theoretical work on African-American liberation. (For precisely that reason, the document appears at the close of the volume.) Indeed, the reader who has not encountered it before might do well to begin with "The Revolutionary Answer," and return to it again after perusing the rest of the book.

The present collection represents a very small portion of a sustained project of research and writing about C. L. R. James which has preoccupied me for several years, and promises to do so for many more. A comprehensive set of acknowledgments is in that case out of the question. But several individuals and institutions have made decisive contributions to work on this volume, and I am pleased to mention them now.

I owe much to the staffs of the Prometheus Research Library (New York), the Walter Reuther Library at Wayne State University (Detroit), and to my former colleagues in the Manuscript Division of the Library of Congress (Washington, D.C.) Jim Murray of the C. L. R. James Institute (New York) has been very gracious in supplying me with copies of James's autobiographical notes from the 1970s. And Kent Worcester provided a photocopy of the "My Friends" pamphlet, now a collector's item.

Paget Henry persuaded me to quit thinking about James's work strictly in terms of the Trotskyist political "field" and to concentrate on cultural questions as well. Of course, Paul Buhle has been saying much the same thing for some years now. He also encouraged me to practice a certain needful and overdue ruthlessness in revising my essay.

Over the years, I have received the occasional friendly call from Edwin Wilson, an independent scholar of black history, inquiring how my work on James was going. He read the various items collected in this volume as I prepared the typescript. His enthusiasm was a tonic reminder that James's "lost writings" really do have an audience. And C. L. R. James would be far more pleased that his essays were being read by one Edwin Wilson (who works for a phone company) than by a dozen professors.

Finally—to save the essential for last—I must acknowledge two women without whom this book would not exist.

In April 1994, Seetha A-Srinivasan asked me to prepare a collection of James's writings for the University Press of Mississippi. She then maintained an extraordinary civility and composure throughout numerous rather mystifying delays.

Rita Tehan, my wife, knows better than anyone just how *critical* a process working on C. L. R. James can be. I use that word for its multitude of nuances, but am thinking in particular of its Greek root: *kairos* ("crisis"). To express gratitude through an etymology is, of course, odd. But Rita understands; and for that, I am more thankful than words can say.

Introduction: The Enigma of Arrival

By the time he came to the United States for a lecture tour in October 1938, C. L. R. James (1901–1989) had begun to make his mark on the world. When he was a child in Trinidad, the conviction took root in him that he must become a writer. His models, his standards, were demanding: Shakespeare's plays, the essays of Hazlitt and Lamb, and the novels of William Makepeace Thackeray, in particular *Vanity Fair*. (By the age of fourteen he had read the book some twenty times, and knew it almost by heart.) Yet this seriousness of purpose could not alter the hard economic fact that, in the Caribbean, there were not enough magazines or buyers of books for James to support himself by his pen. And so, in 1932, he left for Britain. He was thirty-one years old, vastly well read, and blessed with the grace of supreme self-confidence. He also possessed an encyclopedic knowledge of cricket. In Trinidad, he had done a little sports reporting for newspapers. Once settled in London, the famous West Indian batsman Learie Constantine gave him work ghostwriting his autobiography, and the *Manchester Guardian* soon hired James to cover the game. Cricket journalism left plenty of time for politics: by 1934 James had become an adherent of Leon Trotsky's version of Marxism, and he was active in the pan-Africanist circle around George Padmore. He also worked at several ambitious writing projects. In 1936, his drama *Toussaint Louverture*, starring Paul Robeson, played in London to generally good reviews. The same year saw publication of *Minty Alley*, a novel about life among the poor in Trinidad. In 1937, there followed *World Revolution 1917–1936*, a critical history of the Third (Communist) International, written from a Trotskyist perspective. Then, in 1938, James published his masterpiece: *The Black Jacobins*, an account of the slave uprising that created Haiti. His books were issued by Sacker and Warburg. In the 1930s, it was "a midget firm, fragile as bone china," as Fredric Warburg recalled, but it was growing.[1] It was also the press that published George Orwell. *The Black Jacobins* appeared the same year as *Homage to Catalonia*, Orwell's report from the trenches of the Spanish Civil War.

The most vivid portrait of James during the 1930s comes from Fredric Warburg, who deftly conveys the impression his author made in literary and political circles:

> A dark-skinned West Indian Negro from Trinidad, he stood six feet three inches in his socks and was noticeably good-looking. His memory was extraordinary. He could quote, not only passages from the Marxist classics but long extracts from Shakespeare, in a soft lilting English which was a delight to hear. Immensely amiable, he loved the fleshpots of capitalism, fine cooking, fine clothes, fine furniture, and beautiful women, without a trace of the guilty remorse to be expected from a seasoned warrior of the class war. He was brave. Night after night he would address meetings in London and the provinces, denouncing the crimes of the blood-thirsty Stalin, until he was hoarse and his voice a mere croaking in the throat. The Communists who heckled him would have torn him from limb to limb, had it not been for the ubiquity of the police and their insensitivity to propaganda of any hue.[2]

He was a gentleman, then, and a revolutionary. Leaving for America, C. L. R. James expected to return before the next cricket season began.

As in Britain, so again in the United States, James's impact on audiences was dramatic. Shortly after arriving, he gave a lecture to the group of New York intellectuals around the cultural journal *Partisan Review*. The journal's politics were resolutely hostile to the official Communist movement, from which it had recently broken. James appeared before his audience as the author of the first book-length critique of the Communist International in English; his translation of Boris Souvarine's *Stalin* was due from Secker and Warburg in 1939. The talk he gave to the *Partisan Review* group impressed them: one listener suggested that James might be the best speaker the Trotskyists (who had their share of good orators) had yet produced.[3]

Nor did Trotsky's American following waste him. In late November 1938, they organized a meeting where James discussed "The Twilight of the British Empire." It was a *tour de force*. Speaking for three hours without notes, James quoted statistics and historical facts from memory, weaving in allusions to news from the day's newspaper. Listeners were spellbound: a member of the audience compared James to "a great actor, delivering a famous oration."[4] But one can imagine the added impact on an American audience of James, with his British accent and graceful manner, denouncing colonial rule—especially in Africa, where, he said, "British imperialism has for years exercised a tyranny comparable only to fascism. Hitler had little to invent in the methods and techniques of fascist oppression."[5]

While in Harlem, James met with writers and activists, many of whom had been close to the Communist Party. He showed them *The Spark*, a publication of South African supporters of the Fourth International (Trotsky's movement). He also distributed copies of *International African Opinion*, the anti-imperialist journal sponsored by the International African Service Bureau, with which he worked in London. In New York James attended meetings of the Trotskyist organization, and prepared for a national lecture tour. Starting out in Philadelphia on January 6, he made his way to New Haven and to Boston. Over the following weeks, he visited cities in Ohio and Michigan. He alternated between talks on the impending collapse of the British Empire and on "Socialism and the Negro." (At some point during the tour, the two speeches seem to have fused into one: "The Negro People and World Imperialism.") He spent a week in Chicago, where, debating pacifism with the prominent philosopher and lecturer Bertrand Russell, James made a powerful argument for socialist revolution as the only alternative to world war. By a vote of the audience, James won the debate.[6]

several hundred listeners, "some of whom were standing along the walls and crowding the doorways." After the minister made some opening remarks, James took the podium. Aware that most of his listeners would have to get up for work early the next morning, he announced that the lecture would be no more than forty-five minutes long. And it was—exactly. Speaking extemporaneously, but with two months of almost daily practice behind him, James was in complete command of his material.

"The ideas seemed to develop as he went along," writes Constance Webb. "While he spoke, they evolved to completion and created a feeling of participation during the process." The effect was electrifying:

> Towards the end of his speech, the Blacks in the audience began to respond, their voices punctuating each telling point. The words met half-buried ideas, which had been struggling to emerge. Here was the broad, wide world of imagination and heart. Here was an international movement: he linked our activities on the West Coast with those of people in Europe, the Caribbean, and Africa. . . . The summary began and the voices rose around him, timed and framed like a musical passage.

C. L. R.'s eyes gleamed and his face showed that the audience was giving him something vital, as if he were learning from it.[7]

Concept and emotion met, and fused: deep connections were being made. It was evidence of more than mere oratorical ability. For James was not only a skilled speaker. He was also (what is much rarer) a good listener. Exploring the country, he asked questions incessantly. He read the newspapers, with special attention to the African-American press, which opened onto a world scarcely acknowledged in white periodicals. And for the first time since leaving Trinidad in early 1932, James found himself facing a black *society*: one that was stratified and complex, sharing common experiences and problems, yet internally divided along lines of class and caste and ideology.

In late March 1939, after a brief rest, James made his way from California to Mexico to take care of some important political business. In early May, he headed back to the United States. And then something strange happened.

The May 2 issue of *Socialist Appeal*, the Trotskyist newspaper, noted that C. L. R. James would lecture on "The Coming War" in Washington, D.C., the following evening. But in fact May 3 was the very day that James returned to the United States—entering the country, this time, through New Orleans—so that it was impossible for him to be in Washington that night.

Was it, perhaps, simply a mistake on the part of the newspaper? So one might imagine, and dismiss the errant ad from mind, if not for an interesting fact. The notice in the *Appeal* marks a kind of disappearance. It was the last public mention, for many years to come, of C. L. R. James. He remained in the United States. He wrote. He lectured. He kept asking questions. And yet throughout the next decade James became—to borrow the title of a novel by one associate from those years—an invisible man.

What happened? The writings collected in the present volume form part of the answer. But in some ways, they only deepen the enigma. In later years, James came to regard his time in the United States as "the most important years of my life, intellectually and personally. . . . the high water mark . . . ."[8] This was a period of curious intensity, and calls to mind a remark by W. E. B. Du Bois: "It is as though Nature needs make men narrow in order to give them force."[9]

The contours of this chapter in James's biography can be sketched quickly. In March 1939, he was granted a six-month extension on his visa. During the final week of 1940 he registered as an alien with the Immigration and Naturalization Service—which, it seems, promptly lost track of him. For the next dozen years, James worked in the Trotskyist movement, adopting a series of pseudonyms, or "party names." His comrades tended to think of him as "J. R. Johnson." When he lectured, it was to internal meetings of various radical organizations. His writings appeared in the newspapers and other publications of the movement. In time, he came to lead a small Marxist sect of his own, the Johnson-Forest Tendency. ("Forest" was the party name of Trotsky's former secretary, Raya Dunayevskaya.)

The United States government was not particularly happy to discover that it had admitted a black revolutionary. For many years after the authorities finally located him, James faced the prospect of arrest and deportation. By the late 1940s, he was married to an American citizen and had a son; he was setting down roots, and wanted to write a book on the history and cultural significance of American civilization. In 1952, he was imprisoned for several weeks on Ellis Island—along with a number of Communists, also due for expulsion, who cannot have been very pleased to find a "Trotskyite" among them. The following year, his appeal for citizenship again denied, James finally returned to England.

That, in broad outline, is James's trajectory following his disappearance in 1939. We shall return, in a moment, to the details of his life and activity during those years as "underground man."[10] Yet in comprehending this phase of James's life, biographical particulars may count less, perhaps, than the sheer fact and duration of the detour itself. In the prime of his career, at the height of his powers, James drastically changed course. He sacrificed the pleasures of public life to follow the arcane protocols of the far left. His energies were on theoretical debates within small Marxist groups, seemingly far from the mainstream of American life. And yet that is only part of the story. James was also fascinated by the details of ordinary life in the United States—its social diversity and its popular culture (movies, comic strips, sports) as well as the country's sheer size. During his travels, James looked out of his train window upon "the apparently endless miles, hour after hour. . . . I experienced a sense of expansion which has permanently altered my attitude to the world."[11] It was a season of concentration and reorientation, of studying Hegel and Marx and preparing for world revolution, but also of absorbing as much as possible of the scene before him.

The documents gathered in this book show the development of his thinking about one abiding concern, political and personal, from those years: "the Negro question." That expression sounds almost quaint today, and not simply because the word "Negro" has passed out of general usage. The phrase has a slightly nineteenth-century feel, recalling the day when "the woman question" or "the Jewish question" preoccupied social critics. A much closer source was "the national question"—an expression from Marxist political discourse, given currency by Lenin's writings on the colonial revolution. In James's radical milieu, "the Negro question" connoted a very specific set of theoretical and practical problems. Did black people in the United States constitute a national minority? Did black workers share the same interests as the white proletariat? How should the (white) labor movement respond to African-American demands for equality? Was meaningful equality even *possible* under capitalism? And how should socialists relate to existing African-American organizations and institutions?

James had been thinking about related matters for years. "The race question," he wrote in *The Black Jacobins*, "is subsidiary to the class question in politics, and to think of imperialism in terms of race is disastrous. But to neglect the racial factor as merely incidental is an error only less grave than to make it fundamental."[12] His attention had been focused mainly on the colonial movements of the Caribbean and Africa. But the condition and the demands of African-Americans were different. He could use the same analytical tools to frame "the Negro question" in the United States: Marxism was for James the framework through which social movements had to be understood. Yet Marxist theory had almost completely omitted black history and culture from its conceptions of modern society. In the early years of the Communist International, Lenin had directed the attention of Marxists in the United States to the situation of African-Americans, and his writings inspired and instructed James's thinking. But by no means did he make some cookie-cutter application of the Russian's ideas. James tried to bring together Marxist concepts and the history of African-American movements; each must stretch to incorporate the other's insights.

During his stay in the United States, James worked out a thoroughgoing critique of Trotskyism, and sought to reformulate his understanding of Marxism in new terms. This course of study and argument culminated in three book-length works—*Notes on Dialectics* (1948), *Notes on American Civilization* (1950), and *State Capitalism and World Revolution* (1950)—which had very restricted circulation at the time.[13] Within this ambitious enterprise of rethinking Marxist theory, James's writings on "the Negro question" form one discrete series.

Yet answering that "question" was, in itself, a project of many parts: through numerous political documents, pamphlets, newspaper pieces, and essays, James considered the history, culture, and social dynamics of African-American life.

These texts form perhaps the most accessible portion of James's work during his American sojourn. If, over the intervening years, they have been largely ignored, the reasons are not difficult to see. James published his work in radical newspapers and magazines. Other writings circulated in the internal discussion bulletins of small Trotskyist organizations. (Issued in editions of a few hundred mimeographed copies, these bulletins are now rare, and often very fragile.) All of his work appeared under pseudonyms—most frequently "J. R. Johnson," but also "A.A.B.," "W. F. Carlton," "J. Meyer," and "G. F. Ecsktein," among others. In any case, the disguise didn't help. Eventually the FBI determined who "Johnson" and "Meyer" were. And no doubt the writings gathered in the present collection found their way into the appropriate dossiers.

II.

It would be a mistake, if an understandable one, to take for granted the fact that C. L. R. James decided to write about "the Negro question" during his American sojourn. Race played a more complex role than one might suppose in James's conception of himself as a writer. Perhaps the most salient treatment of this matter comes, appropriately enough, from Derek Walcott, a Trinidadian poet. "I think that it must have been extremely difficult and perhaps even painful for James to be seen as a black intellectual," Walcott has said. " . . . [T]he biggest problem of his generation was to have been so brilliant and yet to have been thought of as a brilliant *black* man. That is how he was seen, and it was very hard for him to accept."[14] And indeed, for James, a sense of racial status or identity crystallized only late in life, and under pressure. Until his early thirties, he had lived in Trinidad, a predominantly black island; when recounting the occasional brush with white racism while growing up, James emphasized how little effect such experiences had on him. In England during the 1930s, he found that his color made him at times an object of hatred but also of curiosity. Living in the United States, however, obliged James to become aware of himself—at some heightened pitch of self-consciousness—as black.

"James cannot be compared with other writers such as James Baldwin or Langston Hughes," as Walcott puts it, "because the intellect is different." It certainly was. Early in his stay in the United States, James noted that Americans, black as well as white, "are often hostile to educated West Indian Negroes who from their British education and the comparative absence of sharp racial discrimination in the West Indies are accused, and justly, of having a 'superior' and 'white' attitude."[15] And a very striking passage in a document by one of James's closest political collaborators describes him as an intellectual "of European background theoretically" who brought to his politics "both the knowledge of Marxism and of European civilization."[16]

So James approached questions about race in America as an outsider, by birth and by temperament. His writing seeks to bridge (even though James himself could not cross) a deeply felt sense of cultural and psychological distance. James negotiated those differences through texts composed in a particular vocabulary (that of Marxist theory) and a very specific political context (namely, the American Trotskyist movement).

In a memorandum prepared for a political discussion within the Socialist Workers Party, James averred that he "was not especially interested in the Negro work of the SWP" when he arrived in the United States. Yet circumstances obliged him to pay attention to it:

> A few conversations here and there in Harlem, and some reading, soon made it quite clear that in the American Negro community were the social and political preconditions for a tremendous activity by a revolutionary party. The Communist Party's Negro battalions were going to pieces; yet the [Trotskyist] party leadership, which was supposed to be moving from narrow propaganda to mass agitation, was entirely oblivious of all this. . . .

James "immediately began to study, to make contacts, and to prepare some sort of outline to remedy an absolutely impossible situation. Why had the party leadership not thought about the Negro question at all?"[17]

Without realizing it, James had located a sore spot in the relations between the Russian revolutionary and the American Trotskyists. Writing to his American comrades in 1928, Trotsky insisted: "We must find the road to the most deprived, the darkest strata of the proletariat, beginning with the Negro, whom capitalist society has converted into a pariah, and who must learn to see in us his revolutionary brothers. And this depends wholly upon our energy and devotion to the work."[18] The American Trotskyists had just been expelled from the Communist Party; at the time, they numbered only a few dozen members. Finding a "road to the proletariat" chiefly meant trying to influence—and when possible, to recruit from—the much larger Communist Party. In 1929, the Communist International declared that America's southern states constituted a "Black Belt" where, following the revolution, an independent black state would be created. (The party even distributed maps showing the borders of this nation-to-be.) To the Trotskyists, this seemed one more case of the Communist Party accepting an arbitrary and bureaucratic diktat from Moscow. As an alternative, they proposed slogans calling for "social, political, and economic equality for the Negroes."[19]

To the American Trotskyists' surprise, they learned that Leon Trotsky himself regarded these demands as merely reformist. At a meeting in 1933, the Russian exile admitted the limits of his knowledge about African-Americans. He even wondered if, in the South, they might not speak their own language, which they had been forced to conceal when whites were around. Without advocating the "Black Belt" policy, Trotsky remained open to the possibility that, in their struggle against white oppression, African-Americans might yet emerge as a distinct national minority. He was in any case emphatic that the Trotskyists' approach to black liberation must not subordinate it to the overall class struggle. The white proletariat was, Trotsky noted, overwhelmingly racist. And in a country "so economically mature" as the United States, the revolutionary process might develop rapidly, and take unexpected forms:

> It is then possible that the Negroes will become the most advanced section. We have already a similar example in Russia. The Russians were the European [equivalent of the] Negroes. It is very possible that the Negroes also through the self-determination will proceed to the proletarian dictatorship in a couple of gigantic strides, ahead of the great bloc of white workers. They will then furnish the vanguard. I am absolutely sure that they will in any case fight better than the white workers.[20]

As one scholar of Trotsky's work puts it, his remarks in this 1933 discussion leave "the impression of reading the words of a contemporary proponent of Black Power."[21]

But throughout the 1930s, the American organization never shared Trotsky's assessment of black liberation as central to their work. Meanwhile, the Communists became a formidable presence within the African-American community, particularly through legal support of the "Scottsboro boys." Many party supporters were sincere and courageous fighters for civil rights, and no other multiracial radical organization approached its influence on African-American life. Still, black members often discovered that its advocacy of civil rights was shot through with a profound manipulativeness. The Communist Party was not averse to pronouncing certain figures as "leaders of the Negro people"—the definitive (and sometimes only) qualification for that title evidently being a willingness to follow the party line. And in one instance, the party's unwavering adherence to Soviet foreign policy was particularly disillusioning to African-American supporters. When the U.S.S.R. sold oil to Italy during Mussolini's invasion of Ethiopia, the party denounced all criticism as "counterrevolutionary." But discontented African-American Communists seldom looked to the Trotskyists for an alternative. If they did, there was little evidence of practical activity around racial problems by Trotskyist organizations, which had ceded the field to the numerically far larger Communist Party. And given the profound but unresolved differences with Trotsky himself, the American movement did very little theoretical work on "the Negro question."

This, then, was the situation James found upon arriving in the United States in 1938. Synthesizing his observations, James "prepared a document of no great profundity—how could it be?—and submitted it to Trotsky . . . ." That document, "Preliminary Notes on the Negro Question," largely avoided what James later called "the sterile question of self-determination."[22] He did not debate the Black Belt question, and dismissed without much consideration the whole notion that African-Americans were a distinct national minority.

Yet James did propose that the Trotskyists help build an independent and militant (but nonsocialist) African-American organization. James presented this idea to Trotsky during a series of discussions in Mexico in April 1939. He pointed to the rapid growth of Marcus Garvey's "Back to Africa" movement during the post-World War I period as an indication of the potential for independent, militant, and potentially revolutionary organizations to appear among black Americans. The Garveyite program of repatriation was, James agreed, hopelessly inadequate, judged by Marxist standards. But it approximated a revolutionary program for black people—and was understood as such at the time, James argued, given that

> the Negroes who followed him did not believe for the most part that they were really going back to Africa. We know that those in the West Indies

who were following him had not the slightest intention of going back to Africa, but they were glad to follow a militant leadership. And there is the case of the black woman who was pushed by a white woman in a street car and said to her, "You wait until Marcus gets into power and all you people will be treated in the way you deserve." Obviously she was not thinking of Africa.[23]

As the transcript reveals, the discussion between Trotsky and James was not one between master and disciple. Nor was it a debate. Rather, a genuine dialogue took place. Over the following years, James's thinking on a host of questions began to depart from Trotsky's; yet those 1939 conversations remained central to the development of James's work on African-American matters.

Following the discussion in Mexico, James went back to the United States in early May 1939. As noted, this seems to have been the beginning of his existence as "underground man." But his arrival in New Orleans also marked a crucial moment in James's experience of the United States. Friends had tried to dissuade him from travelling by himself. James knew about the social code governing race relations in the American South. He assured the comrades that he wasn't planning to foment revolution; he just wanted to see things for himself. He felt "a slight nervousness" before reaching New Orleans, and contemplated "how terribly the minds and characters of [American] Negroes must be affected" by life in the South, "especially those with no experience or political or historical background to help them, or no consciousness of a way out."[24] James steeled himself for the experience. But reading the newspapers and the novels of William Faulkner had scarcely prepared him for the world of Jim Crow.

Needing a ride, James held his hand out in the street to hail a cab. One finally stopped, a short distance away. The white driver paid no attention to James. He stood in the street, confused, until a black boy finally explained that the cab wouldn't pick him up, and that he might well get run over if he tried again. Over the next few days, the young man served as James's guide to New Orleans and to life behind the color bar. He could only eat in certain restaurants, for example. He knew that, on a bus, segregation restricted black riders to the last three rows. But fellow passengers in the back had to explain another rule: if the bus were crowded, a white person standing beside your seat expected you to give it up.

The nuances of segregation were puzzling at first, but the frustration of it all soon turned to anger—and to anxiety. Walking down the street, he became uncomfortably aware that women were looking at him. That was nothing new: James was handsome. In other cities, he might enjoy female attention or ignore it, depending on his mood. In New Orleans, though, racial tensions made this impossible: "The white young women fastened their eyes on me in a way that had me very embarrassed. I made no counter-move. I was scared. . . ."[25] He returned north by bus, with his trip through the South providing a deeper immersion in the realities of Jim Crow. Once settled back in New York, James "wouldn't talk to anyone from the party for several days," as a fellow Trotskyist recalled.[26] (Those party members were presumably white.)

Upon recovering from the trip, James worked to prepare for the national convention of the Socialist Workers Party in early July 1939. On the basis of the discussions with Trotsky, James drafted two resolutions that the convention accepted.[27] Without raising a call for a separate black state, the party would affirm the *right* of the African-American people to national self-determination, if they so chose, in the course of the revolutionary process. The party established a National Negro Department, with James directing its work. A call for office supplies went out. James wrote a column titled "The Negro Question" for *The Socialist Appeal*, and conducted a well-attended class on black history. Within a few months, the party had re-cruited about thirty new African-American members. And the Communists rewarded these efforts: as James noted, the party "[did] us the honor of carrying on a furious campaign in its classes on Negro work against the 'Trotskyite line' on the Negro question."[28]

In Mexico, Trotsky asked an American visitor about James's work. He was very satisfied to hear in reply that the Negro Department "was going night and day."[29] But this promising beginning soon came to a halt. As World War II approached, Trotsky's followers began to argue over the nature of the Soviet Union. Trotsky maintained that "the gains of the October Revolution," especially nationalized industry and central planning, had to be defended against both the Stalinist bureaucracy and foreign capitalists. James was among those who argued that the Soviet system had become a kind of class society and therefore not worthy of support by revolutionaries. Throughout the winter of 1939–40, the movement's attentions turned inward. James continued to write about black issues for *Socialist Appeal*, and the December 1939 issue of its theoretical journal, *New International*, was devoted to articles on "the Negro question." Like everyone else in the organization, though, he was caught up in the dispute with Trotsky as the Socialist Workers Party moved inexorably towards a split.[30]

By April 1940, James left to help found a new Trotskyist group called the Workers Party. (As *Partisan Review* editor and founding party member Dwight Macdonald later put it, originality of nomenclature was never the movement's strong point.) In this now much smaller pond, James became a still bigger fish. He wrote extensively for the new party's press, including tributes to Marcus Garvey and Leon Trotsky (both of whom died in 1940), two pieces on *Native Son* by Richard Wright, and a study of "Imperialism in Africa."[31] The strain of turning out countless pages of copy for the Workers Party may have aggravated the stomach ulcer that chronically bothered James. But a brief period of hospitalization gave him the opportunity to begin studying *Capital* more closely; and in early 1941, James produced an extensive document interpreting the Soviet Union as a society fundamentally identical to capitalism as Marx had described it.[32] With a handful of others who accepted this analysis, James became the head of the "state capitalist" minority that emerged at the Workers Party national convention in September 1941.[33]

Just after the convention, James headed back to the South, this time to Missouri. Trotskyists there had been working with sharecroppers who were preparing to strike for higher pay. The day he arrived, a threat of violence was in the air. Black parents had been in conflict with the local school over threats to their children. A rumor had it that whites were planning to descend on the black settlement that night. James was shuttled off to a safer area for the time being; the sharecroppers stood guard with guns, just in case the rumor turned out to be true. It didn't, but over the next several months, as he travelled throughout the region, James grew accustomed to seeing weaponry. This was the class struggle in the flesh. His accent made James rather conspicuous, and Workers Party organizers wanted to keep him from becoming too visible. For several months James divided his time between St. Louis and the back roads of southeast Missouri. And when the time came for the strike, James sat down with the croppers and prepared a pamphlet explaining their demands and strategy. He also wrote a series of reports on the movement for *Labor Action* newspaper.[34]

At the end of the summer in 1942, not long after returning from southeast Missouri, James again fell seriously ill. His ulcer grew worse, and in December it perforated; he collapsed in the street outside a movie theater. He was rushed to the hospital for an operation.[35] This helped, but did not cure, the problem. Confined to bed for long periods, James went back to working out the implications of his concept of Soviet state-capitalism, while also reading widely in American history and literature. He found it difficult to write during his illness, but managed to dictate numerous articles and theoretical documents. And he began corresponding with Constance Webb, a young actress he had met in California some time before, and with whom he had fallen in love.[36]

No doubt to the puzzlement of his comrades, James also developed a fascination with radio serials. He tuned in regularly to the soap operas, conscious that this dramatic form, listened to by millions of women throughout the country, answered some need.[37] Unable to participate so readily in political activity as he had before surgery, James was nonetheless developing a sense of cultural politics very unlike anything typical of Leninist party norms.

This hardly meant that he was leaving those norms behind. By 1943, some fifteen or twenty people in the Workers Party had accepted James's analysis of the Soviet Union. They also shared his perspective on "the independent Negro struggle," rejecting any suggestion that black freedom movements required the leadership of the white labor unions. The small group became known (rather inevitably) as "the Johnsonites," after James's most frequently used pseudonym. Organized as a faction within the Workers Party, the Johnsonite minority argued for alternative policies and criticized the leadership on a variety of fronts.[38] It also functioned as a kind of study circle:

> We struggled to understand Marx in the light of European history and civilization, reading *Capital* side by side with Hegel's *Logic* in order to get a sense of dialectical and historical materialism. We explored the world of Shakespeare, of Beethoven, of Melville, Hawthorne, and the Abolitionists, of Marcus Garvey and Pan-Africanism. At the same time most of us worked in the plant, struggling to squeeze every ounce of revolutionary significance out of what American workers were saying and doing.[39]

At the war's end, James's circle had emerged as the main oppositional current within the Workers Party. The group remained tiny: at its peak, the Johnson minority had between seventy and eighty members, out of some five hundred in the party as a whole. Yet the importance of this small organization to James cannot be overstated, and not simply because it was his base of political support within the international Trotskyist movement.[40] The group also became his window on a country he was beginning to think of as his own. The faction attracted a few intellectuals, some young radicals, and a number of factory workers, black and white. It formed a loose network, with Johnsonite circles in Workers Party branches in New York, Philadelphia, Detroit, Los Angeles, and elsewhere. And as the Johnsonites read Hegel and Frederick Douglass, or discussed the postwar strike wave, James, in turn, studied the American personality through them.

Factional activity, plus a long-distance romance with Constance Webb (who lived in Los Angeles), obliged James to travel a great deal. But in New York, he lived "on the border between Harlem and the white community." This had become a matter of necessity: in a predominately white area, the large number of his black visitors would have been too conspicuous, and vice versa. As James put it, "I usually lived somewhere in between where blacks and whites were living, so that my visitors would not be particularly noticeable, either to my neighbors or to the police." He also frequented Greenwich Village, in particular a restaurant called The Calypso, where radical intellectuals of all races gathered alongside artists and stage performers. One of the waiters was a young writer named James Baldwin, then at work on his first novel; Baldwin's friend Stan Weir (The Calypso's dishwasher) was a Workers Party member and Johnsonite sympathizer. The Calypso's regulars shared the feeling, in Weir's words, "that the heads of state in both Russia and the United States were incapable of leading the world to more personal freedom and were part of the problem." It was a place "where people were genuinely entertaining each other, and as an extension of their enjoyment, discussing politics."[41]

Another very serious discussion was James's ongoing conversation with the novelist Richard Wright. They had met not long after James arrived in the United States, but seem to have maintained a certain distance throughout the early 1940s—an effect, no doubt, of the pressure of their respective political allegiances. Wright had been a member of the Communist Party since the mid-1930s, though his relationship with the party was often strained. In 1942, Wright left the party when it quit providing legal assistance to challenges to racial discrimination. Even so, Wright kept his criticisms of the party to himself. It was only in 1944—after completing an autobiographical manuscript, later published as *American Hunger*, which included a very sharp account of his relationship with the Communists—that Wright and James became more than casual acquaintances.

Wright, James said, "had read my books, had heard me speak, knew that I was a deadly enemy of what he so passionately believed in. But we became more and more friendly."[42] James later claimed that "never for one single moment did [he] try to influence [Wright] in a new political direction." This seems a little implausible. James had been arguing against the Communists for so many years that it scarcely seems imaginable he would temper his criticisms just to be polite. And one historian has suggested that James may have influenced Wright finally to go public with his criticisms of the Communist Party.[43]

In any case, during a conversation in mid-1944 Wright and James discovered that—coming though they did from very different backgrounds in the Stalinist and Trotskyist camps—they had reached the same understanding of "the Negro question." In a letter to Constance Webb, James gave the gist of their shared perspective:

> Briefly, the idea is this, that the Negro is "nationalist" to the heart and is perfectly right to be. His racism, his nationalism, are a necessary means of giving him strength, self-respect, and organization *in order to fight for integration into American society*. It is a perfect example of dialectical contradiction. Further, however, the Negroes represent a force in the future development of American society out of all proportion to their numbers. The repression has created such frustration that this, when socially motivated, will become one of the most powerful social forces in the country.[44]

James became part of the circle of black intellectuals Wright considered his "thinking coterie," along with Ralph Ellison, Horace Cayton, and E. F. Frazier. Spurred on by the surprising commercial and critical success of Gunnar Myrdal's enormous sociological study *An American Dilemma: The Negro Problem and Modern Democracy* (1944), Wright planned to edit a collection of writings provisionally titled *The Negro Speaks*. An essay by James, "The American Negro Looks at History," would be paired with one by the poet Melvin Tolson, "History Looks at the American Negro." And Eric Williams—James's former student, later the prime minister of Trinidad— would write a chapter called "The Negro's Strength and Weakness."[45]

Unfortunately the project collapsed.[46] So did plans to launch a journal, *American Pages*, to be subtitled "A magazine reflecting a minority mood. Nonpartisan, nonpolitical, espousing no current creed, ideology, or organization."[47] But James's relationship with Wright was more than professional, and throughout the mid-1940s the men were frequent guests in each other's homes. (James later wryly noted that his friend fancied himself a cook, a point he chose not to question.) When Constance Webb joined them, James had a sharp reminder that he was not an American:

> [S]oon they would begin to talk animatedly. One of them had read some statement about Negroes in some newspaper or some book. We had been to eat somewhere and the waiter had been either offensive or had gone out of his way to show that he was on our side. Matters of this kind occupied them unceasingly, and I found myself left out. Many of the things they saw I did not see, and if I saw them paid little attention. Dick was a man of wide reading and an extremely profound analyst of society. . . . Constance was a wide reader and serious student. But I did not, could not, take part in what so preoccupied them. I had grown up in a different environment.[48]

James's education in the details of race in American life, which had begun on the streets of New Orleans a few years before, was ongoing.

It is an irony of some import that, by the mid-1940s, James found himself much closer to an ex-Communist (but decidedly non-Trotskyist) writer than he did to most of his comrades in the Workers Party. Within the party, James was derided as an ultraleftist and an eccentric. Max Shachtman, the head of the party, often referred to him as a "literary man"—not, after all, a compliment in the Bolshevik lexicon. The Johnsonite study groups on Hegel and *Capital* seemed especially peculiar: a sign that Johnsonite politics were "in the stratosphere." Particularly hostile was Ernest Rice McKinney, the other leading black member of the party. He gave James the nickname "Sportin' Life," after the pimp-like villain in Gershwin's opera *Porgy and Bess*. Sportin' Life is a drug dealer, pushing "happy dust" (read: revolutionary delusions) and enjoying "the high life" in New York. In the number "It Ain't Necessarily So," he sings:

> Sun ain't got no shame, moon ain't got no shame
> So I ain't got no shame, doin' what I like to do!

Nor was this simply a matter of personal animosity. Writing for the Workers Party majority, McKinney upheld a view of African-American struggles directly opposed to the position developed by James: "The white worker must take the lead and offensive in the struggle for the Negro's democratic rights. . . . The white workers are strongly organized, they have had ages of experience and they are powerful. On the other hand, no matter how great their courage and determination, the Negroes are organizationally, financially and numerically weak in comparison with the white workers, and woefully and pitifully weak in the face of present-day capitalism. . . ."[49]

In 1947, the Johnsonites left the Workers Party to rejoin the Socialist Workers Party, which proved much more receptive to James's conception of the independent black struggle. The SWP was "orthodox Trotskyist" and so an unlikely place for James and his cothinkers. By the time he returned to the SWP, James's ideas were in many ways becoming closer to those of European Marxists (e.g., Anton Pannekoek or Karl Korsch) who, in the 1920s, had criticized Lenin and Trotsky from the left. Yet the SWP upheld not only Trotsky's analysis of the U.S.S.R. (with which the Johnsonites disagreed) but also the policy on "the Negro question" that had taken shape during the 1939 discussions in Mexico. Over the intervening years, the SWP had published more pamphlets on the black struggle than on any other topic. And it participated in a number of campaigns:

> The SWP was the only political group to join with Black organizations to defend 15 African-American sailors court-martialed in 1940 for protesting segregation in the Navy. In 1942, the SWP played a leading role in defense efforts for Black sharecropper Odell Waller, who was legally lynched in the state of Virginia for acting in self-defense against his white landlord. In 1946 the party organized a campaign against the Ku Klux Klan after a Black family was burned to death in Fontana, California. During the same year, the SWP was involved in a fight against police brutality; the victims were the Ferguson brothers of Freeport, New York. A successful campaign to free James Hickman from a Chicago prison took place in 1947; Hickman had killed his landlord in the belief that the man was responsible for the death of Hickman's children in a slum fire.[50]

And in the years since the 1940 split, the SWP had almost tripled in size. Among its recruits was a sizable cohort of new black members. While not the only (or even the decisive) factor in the decision by James and his associates to fuse with the SWP, this record certainly made the party a more attractive place to work.

After the fusion, James was asked to prepare a resolution on "the Negro question" for the SWP. That resolution—"Negro Liberation Through Revolutionary Socialism," accepted at the party's national convention in July 1948—was more or less a revised and condensed version of James's "Historical Development of the Negroes in American Society" (1943).[51] But in presenting the document to the convention, James delivered a lecture that summed up, in clear and precise fashion, the conclusions he had reached after a decade of activity and writing on African-American politics. In the years ahead, James would point to "The Revolutionary Answer to the Negro Problem in the United States" as the culmination of his thinking on the matter.

For some in his audience, the speech was a memorable event as well. At the convention, black members met in an informal caucus to discuss their grievances. While the SWP had successfully recruited African-Americans, some whites in the group remained chauvinistic towards them; in a few branches, there had been incidents displaying real hostility and racism towards black members and contacts. As one black SWP member recalled, when James got up to speak, there was an expectation that he would, as a leader, try to "smooth over" the race question. But "The Revolutionary Answer" seemed to address the tensions within the party itself, and to present a way forward:

> When I listened to this leader's general presentation, I felt I was floating someplace. What really got me was when he said that no Negro, especially Negroes below the Mason and Dixon line, ever believed that their problems would be solved by writing or telegraphing Congress. He went on to say that "the Negroes' independent struggle had a vitality and a validity of its own." . . . The convention accepted the Negro resolution. I felt good. Now we had something, something to go by.[52]

But at the very time these theses on black liberation were being accepted by the SWP, James was breaking utterly with Trotskyism itself, whether "orthodox" or otherwise. In *Notes on Dialectics* (1948) and *State Capitalism and World Revolution* (1950), James abandoned the Leninist model of the revolutionary party, and in 1951, his cothinkers left the SWP to form an independent Marxist organization, the Committees of Correspondence. Following James's expulsion from the United States in 1953, this small group would suffer two splits of its own.[53]

However, the SWP continued to base its work in support of African-American liberation on the 1939 discussions in Mexico and the 1948 conventions documents. And so James continued to have some influence among the Trotskyists well after leaving the movement. When the SWP began working with Malcolm X in the mid-1960s, Conrad Lynn (a civil rights lawyer and a friend of James's) gave Malcolm copies of James's writings—including, almost certainly, a pamphlet containing "The Revolutionary Answer."

As Lynn recalled, the first time they discussed James, Malcolm "talked about James as an orator." By that time, James had long been out of the country. "I don't know where [Malcolm] learned about that," Lynn said.[54] It was evidence, perhaps, that information may circulate underground, only to emerge in the most unlikely, yet appropriate, places.

I I I .

Gathering this selection of writings from a distinct period and quarter of C. L. R. James's life, I have had the sensation, time and again, of piecing together the fragments of a single book. The reader must decide whether or not the parts add up to an integral whole. As an editor I am, of course, biased. Yet James himself was highly conscious of the process by which he worked out his own thinking on a given topic. It seems to me that his writings on the Marxist interpretation of "the Negro question" constitute an instance of the process of observation, hypothesis-making, research, and speculation he described in *Notes on Dialectics* (1948). In the process of working out an idea, James would prepare "an article or a thesis." But that moment of synthesis became, in turn, an incentive to rethink his conclusions and to seek (in a distinctively Jamesian phrase) "to co-relate logic and history."

> You are sure of the end only when you can trace the thing stage by stage, the dialectical development accounting for all the major historical facts. Sometimes you can work backwards. I remember telling [Raya Dunayevskaya] one day, "Go and read Populism and search for an in-dependent Negro movement. It ought to be there." She found it in a few hours, over a million Negroes, buried and forgotten. Over and over again I have to look for an important missing link or links. If I cannot find them, I have to give up the theses and find another. If you read how Marx wrote *Capital* you will see he wrote it, a draft, then reorganized that. He was searching for the logical movement which embraced all the facts.[55]

Without quite claiming to have reproduced James's approach in the editing of this collection, I should nonetheless indicate that his sense of method—of reflection and revision—guided my efforts to arrange his scattered writings on African-American matters.

The core of the book consists of three major works: "Preliminary Notes on the Negro Question" (1939), "The Historical Development of the Negroes in American Society" (1943), and "The Revolutionary Answer to the Negro Problem in the United States" (1948). Each document represents an effort by James to synthesize his observations, reading, and theoretical perspectives. These are theoretical texts; yet each one also bears some trace of James's personal engagement with the American scene. From first impressions ("Preliminary Notes") to final conceptual summation ("Revolutionary Answer"), these writings form a sequence which, I think, gives this book its structure.

James's theoretical documents were written for an audience of Marxist party cadres. "My Friends" (1940) is a very different sort of text altogether. Printed by the thousands and distributed as widely as possible, the pamphlet is an example of James as revolutionary propagandist. Through the fiction of a black sharecropper taking President Roosevelt's place at the microphone, it parodies mainstream political discourse. The opening poem by Claude McKay was already a classic of black radical literature when the pamphlet appeared. But the verses had another resonance at the time, for Winston Churchill had recently used them to stir the British will to fight. "During the tight little island's finest hour," as Melvin Tolson put it, Churchill "snatched Claude McKay's poem *If We Must Die* from the closet of the Harlem renaissance, and catholicized it before the House of Commons, as if it were the talismanic uniform of His Majesty's field marshal."[56] James's satire, then, seizes the poem back, inserting it once again into the tradition of protest literature.

As Trotskyist party leader, James produced numerous columns and articles for *Socialist Appeal*, *Labor Action*, and *The Militant*. There are scores, possibly hundreds, of these pieces, and no doubt James wrote quite a few more under pseudonyms not yet identified. His abundant journalistic output included a fair quantity of what might be called "revolutionary boilerplate": newspaper columns denouncing racism, capitalist hypocrisy, and the misleaders of the African-American community. At the time, in its original venue, this work was doubtless useful; yet such pieces do not hold up well, especially when read in bulk. I selected a few of James's newspaper writings, with an eye to including the most lively and durable articles, such as the reportage on the struggles of the Missouri sharecroppers, the commentary on the 1943 riots, and some of his cultural journalism.

The series of James's writings on history includes a number of brief newspaper articles, as well as some longer essays published in *New International* magazine. The pieces are arranged to create a sort of historical panorama. Conspicuous, and puzzling, is the absence of any treatment of

Reconstruction. James was deeply impressed and influenced by W. E. B. Du Bois's *Black Reconstruction in America* (1935), and the fact that he seems not to have written anything on the period is in itself very interesting. The review of Eric Williams's *The Negro in the Caribbean* may seem a little anomalous here, among texts concentrating on the United States. But it is a document of considerable interest in illuminating the relation between the authors of *The Black Jacobins* and *Capitalism and Slavery*.

Under the heading "Aspects of Marxist Theory" are gathered three texts reflecting James's concern with questions of dialectics and method. They are organically connected to his work on "the Negro question." But they also serve to connect the present collection to *Notes on Dialectics* (1948) and *State Capitalism and World Revolution* (1950). They may persuade at least a few readers to explore these somewhat more forbidding works of dialectical-materialist theory.

James's thinking on "the Negro question" constitutes a distinct, discrete, yet relatively small portion of an enormous and highly varied body of work. For a broader overview of his life and other writings, the reader who has not yet done so will want to consult Paul Buhle's *C. L. R. James: The Artist as Revolutionary* (1989) and Kent Worcester's *C. L. R. James: A Political Biography* (1996). My own treatment of his American years highlights particular circumstances and details that might illuminate his writings on "the Negro question." And from my study of that often shadowy period of his life, one memory—recalled by James many years later—has held a special fascination for me. It is so striking that I hope it may resonate in the mind of the reader who explores the writings gathered here.

The scene is set in the early 1940s, at the Apollo Theater in Harlem. Visiting it became, one gathers from his recollection, something of a routine for C. L. R. James. And afternoons were a particularly good time to go: tickets were half-price. So imagine James taking his seat at the Apollo. The night before, at a Trotskyist meeting, he had argued some point on the working-class revolution in Europe, or the class nature of the Soviet Union. He may be taking a break from work on a long article for *The New International*—or an even longer theoretical document for a mimeographed discussion bulletin. Perhaps he carries with him one of the two volumes of Hegel's *Science of Logic*, or a heavily-thumbed copy of volume 9 from Lenin's *Selected Works*. Apart from his book, though, he is, at least for a while, alone. But there will be another meeting this evening. (To prepare for revolution requires patience, and many, many meetings).

So James gets comfortable. His mind may wander back to last night's debate, or tonight's. But as the band starts to play, his attention is riveted, though not on the music as such. What he studies is the audience. "Time and again I noticed the extraordinary power that came from them," he would recall. Never before had James seen such a response to a performance. The black crowd didn't care about the race of the artists: "They made no distinctions about whites. Artie Shaw, Benny Goodman, and these others would get the same reception when the music moved [them] as [when] Duke Ellington or Louis Armstrong [played]."

James never went to the Apollo to dance: "I wasn't much of a dancer at any time except when I was much younger." Still, the interaction between band and audience was compelling and found its way, eventually, into James's own writing. The music (or rather, its resonance with the crowd) would be transformed, by some alchemy, into the more severe language of Marxist theoretical documents. The echoes might not be quite audible there any longer. But the audience at the Apollo shaped James's thinking on the African-American struggle as much, in its way, as Lenin's theses on the national question. The response of the listeners was such, James recalled, that he said, "on one or two occasions: 'All the power is hidden in them there. It's waiting to come out. And the day . . . it takes political form, it is going to shake this nation as nothing before has shaken it.' "[57]

1. Fredric Warburg, *All Authors Are Equal: The Publishing Life of Fredric Warburg 1936–1971* (London: Hutchinson, 1973), 1.

2. Fredric Warburg, *An Occupation for Gentlemen* (London: Hutchinson, 1959), 214.

3. Michael Wreszin, *A Rebel in Defense of Tradition: The Life and Politics of Dwight Macdonald* (New York: Basic Books, 1994), 80–81.

4. Frank Lovell, quoted by Paul Le Blanc in the introduction to Scott McLemee and Paul Le Blanc, eds., *C. L. R. James and Revolutionary Marxism: Selected Writings of C. L. R. James 1939–1949* (Atlantic Highlands, N.J.: Humanities Press, 1994), 4.

5. C. L. R. James, "Twilight of the British Empire" (New York local of the Socialist Workers Party, 1938, mimeographed). A copy may be found in the John Dwyer manuscript collection (box 5, folder 18), Walter Reuther Library, Detroit.

6. "James, Russell Debate Capitalist System Before Large Audience," *Socialist Appeal*, 28 February 1939.

7. Constance Webb, "C. L. R. James, the Speaker and His Charisma," in *C. L. R. James: His Life and Work*, ed. Paul Buhle (London: Allison and Busby, 1986), 169–70.

8. C. L. R. James to Lyman and Freddy Paine and Grace (Lee) and Jimmy Boggs, 24 February 1976. My thanks to Paul Buhle for providing me with a copy of this letter.

9. W. E. B. Du Bois, *The Souls of Black Folk* (1903; reprint, New York: Penguin, 1989), 38.

10. In an earlier essay, I wrote: "The characterization of James as 'underground man' appears in 'Johnsonism: A Political Appraisal' (April 1956), a memorandum signed 'O'Brian' (later identified as Peter Mallory) . . . ." I have been informed by Martin Glaberman that "Peter Mallory" was itself merely another pseudonym for John Dwyer, the husband of Raya Dunayevskaya. This naturally raises the question of which man, James or Dwyer, went deeper "underground"!

11. C. L. R. James, *Mariners, Renegades, and Castaways: The Story of Herman Melville and the World We Live In* (1953; reprint, London: Allison & Busby, 1985), 167.

12. C. L. R. James, *The Black Jacobins: Toussaint L'Ouverture and the San Domingo Revolution*, 2d ed. (New York: Vintage Books, 1963), 283.

13. *Notes on Dialectics* (1948) and *Notes on American Civilization* (1950) originally circulated among James's associates in carbon copies, while *State Capitalism and World Revolution* (1950) first appeared as a mimeographed internal bulletin of the Socialist Workers Party. Each work is now available in a commercial edition.

14. Derek Walcott, "A Tribute to C. L. R. James," in *C. L. R. James: His Intellectual Legacies*, ed. Selwyn Cudjoe and William E. Cain (Amherst: University of Massachusetts Press, 1995), 41.

15. C. L. R. James, "Preliminary Notes on the Negro Question," 7.

16. Raya Dunayevskaya, "Our Organization: American Roots and World Concepts" (circa 1953, mimeographed), 15. My thanks to Martin Glaberman for providing a copy of this text from his files.

17. C. L. R. James ("J. R. Johnson"), "Roots of the Party Crisis" (Socialist Workers Party, ca. March 1940, mimeographed), 20. My thanks to Walter Daum for providing me with a copy of this document from his collection.

18. Leon Trotsky, "Tasks of the American Opposition" (1929), quoted in introduction to *Leon Trotsky on Black Nationalism and Self-Determination*, ed. George Breitman (New York: Pathfinder Press, 1972), 5.

19. For a discussion of the American Trotskyist analysis of "the Negro

question" in this early period, see Peter Drucker, *Max Shachtman and His Left: A Socialist's Odyssey through "the American Century"* (Atlantic Highlands: Humanities Press, 1994), 58–61.

20. Leon Trotsky, "The Negro Question in America" (1933), in *Leon Trotsky on Black Nationalism and Self-Determination*, 18.

21. Baruch Knei-Paz, *The Social and Political Thought of Leon Trotsky* (Oxford: Oxford University Press, 1978), 555.

22. C. L. R. James, "Roots of the Party Crisis," 20.

23. Leon Trotsky et al., "Self Determination for the American Negroes" (1939) in *Leon Trotsky on Black Nationalism and Self-Determination*, p. 25.

24. C. L. R. James to Constance Webb, ca. April 1939; quoted in Kent Worcester, *C. L. R. James: A Political Biography* (Albany: State University of New York Press, 1996), p. 58.

25. Details of the visit to New Orleans appear in the unpublished notes for an autobiography James dictated in the 1970s. My thanks to Paul Buhle for allowing me to examine selections from this material, gathered during work on his biography *C. L. R. James: The Artist as Revolutionary* (London: Verso, 1988).

26. B. J. Widick, telephone interview with Kent Worcester, 29 April 1994. My thanks to Kent Worcester for providing a copy of his notes from this conversation.

27. See C. L. R. James, "The SWP and Negro Work" and "The Right of Self-Determination and the Negro in the United States of North America" (both 1939), reprinted in *Leon Trotsky on Black Nationalism and Self-Determination*, 49–55.

28. C. L. R. James, "Roots of the Party Crisis," 20–21.

29. Joseph Hansen, "Trotsky's Last Battle Against the Revisionists," *Fourth International* (November 1940), 166.

30. For a very partisan yet invaluable account of the 1939–40 dispute within the American Trotskyist movement, see James P. Cannon, *The Struggle for a Proletarian Party* (New York: Pathfinder Press, 1943). See also Drucker, *Max Shachtman and His Left*, 106–43, for an account of the split more sympathetic to Trotsky's critics.

31. For the essays on Trotsky, Wright, and Africa, see McLemee and Le Blanc, *C. L. R. James and Revolutionary Marxism*.

32. James first presented his theory in "Stalinist Russia is a Fascist State: Towards a Clarification of the Discussion," in *Workers Party Bulletin* No. 7 (March 1941), under the name "J. R. Johnson." A copy of this document may be found at the Prometheus Research Library (New York, New York).

33. C. L. R. James ("J. R. Johnson"), "Resolution on the Russian Question" in *The Russian Question: Resolutions of the 1941 Convention on the Character of the Russian State*, ed. Ernest Erber (New York: Workers Party, ca. 1941).

34. For more on James's work in southeast Missouri, see Worcester, *C. L. R. James: A Political Biography*, 70–72.

35. C. L. R. James to Constance Webb, postmarked 26 August 1943. Copies of James's correspondence with Webb are on deposit at the Schomberg Library in New York. My thanks to Paul Buhle for sending me copies of several of these letters.

36. Selwyn Cudjoe, " 'As Ever Darling, All My Love': The Love Letters of C. L. R. James," in *C. L. R. James: His Intellectual Legacies*, ed. Cudjoe and Cain, 215–43.

37. On James's preoccupation with American popular culture, see "Letters to Critics" in *The C. L. R. James Reader*, ed. Anna Grimshaw (Cambridge, Mass.: Blackwell, 1992).

38. For an overview of the Johnson-Forest Tendency's trajectory, see the introduction to *C. L. R. James and Revolutionary Marxism*, ed. McLemee and Le Blanc, 8–19.

39. James Boggs and Grace Lee Boggs, "A Critical Reminiscence," in *C. L. R. James: His Life and Work*, ed. Buhle, 178.

40. See the various documents and discussions from the Johnson-Forest Tendency included in *Les congrès de la IV Internationale. Tome 3: Bouleversements et crises de l'après-guerre (1946–1950)*, ed. Rudolphe Prager (Montreuil: Editions le Breche, 1988).

41. Stan Weir, "Meetings with James Baldwin," *Against the Current* (January–February 1989), 35.

42. C. L. R. James, "James Baldwin's Attack on *Native Son*," *Trinidad Guardian Magazine* (23 October 1966), 7.

43. Gerald Horne, *Black Liberation/Red Scare: Ben Davis and the Communist Party* (Newark, Del.: University of Delaware Press, 1993), 109, 353–54.

44. C. L. R. James to Constance Webb. Included in *The C. L. R. James Reader*, ed. Grimshaw, 146–47, where it is dated "1945." Internal evidence clearly shows that this is a mistake: James indicates (1) that Wright is correcting page proofs for his memoir and (2) that Wright is about to break publically with the Communist Party. The page proofs for *Black Boy* (1945) were sent to Wright in May 1944; his article "I Tried to Be a Communist" appeared in the August–September 1944 issue of *Atlantic Monthly*.

45. Michel Fabre, *The Unfinished Quest of Richard Wright*, trans. Isabel Barzun (New York: William Morrow, 1973), 267–68, 581.

46. For a brief discussion of Gunnar Myrdal by James, see "The Negro Question and Public Awareness" in this collection. See also Raya Dunayevskaya ("Freddie Forest"), "Negro Intellectuals in Dilemma: Myrdal's Study of a Crucial Problem," *The New International* (November 1944), 369–72.

47. Constance Webb, *Richard Wright: A Biography* (New York: Putnam, 1968), 220–22. For a brief discussion of similarities between *American Pages* and

the Johnson-Forest newspaper *Correspondence*, see Scott McLemee, "American Civilization and World Revolution: C. L. R. James in the United States, 1938–1953 and Beyond," in *C. L. R. James and Revolutionary Marxism*, ed. McLemee and Le Blanc, 230–32.

48. C. L. R. James, "There are Negroes Who Do Not Feel This Rage," *Trinidad Guardian Magazine* (30 October 1966), 18.

49. Ernest Rice McKinney ("David Coolidge") in "Negroes and the Revolution: Resolution of the Political Committee," *The New International* (January 1945), 10.

50. Evelyn Sell, "How the Concept of the Dual Nature of the African American Struggle Developed," *Bulletin in Defense of Marxism* (December 1982), 8. Sell's article surveys the development of various positions on African-American politics within the American Trotskyist movement.

51. Published in *Fourth International* (May/June 1950).

52. Sy Owens ("Charles Denby"), *Indignant Heart: A Black Worker's Journal* (1952; reprint, Detroit: Wayne State University Press, 1989), 173.

53. In 1955, Raya Dunayevskaya ("Forest") split the group following a conflict precipitated by the pressures of McCarthyism; the issues involved in this break were not political but strictly financial and organizational. A publication of her group, *American Civilization on Trial* (Detroit: News and Letters, 1963), reflects the Johnson-Forest Tendency's work on "the Negro question." (The pamphlet's title is taken from James's 1950 manuscript "Notes on American Civilization.") James's 1962 break with James Boggs and Grace Lee Boggs followed a dispute over the document by James Boggs later published as *The American Revolution: Pages from a Negro Worker's Notebook* (New York: Monthly Review Press, 1963), which abandoned a number of Marxist premises. The Boggses became prominent community activists in Detroit. Despite the catastrophic loss of members, a small Jamesian group called the Facing Reality Publishing Committee survived until 1970. Its pamphlet *Negro Americans Take the Lead: A Statement on the Crisis in American Civilization* (Detroit: Facing Reality, 1964) applies the perspective of James's 1948 resolution to the era of the civil rights movement.

54. Conrad Lynn, telephone interview with Paul Buhle. My thanks to Paul Buhle for sharing with me his notes from this interview.

55. C. L. R. James, *Notes on Dialectics: Hegel, Marx, Lenin* (1948; reprinted, London: Allison & Busby, 1980), 204.

56. Melvin Tolson, review (unpublished?) of *Selected Poems of Claude McKay*. Undated typescript in the Melvin Tolson Collection, Box 4, Library of Congress.

57. C. L. R. James, undated notes. Thanks to Jim Murray for sending me a number of pages from this unpublished project.

C. L. R. James on the 'Negro Question'

ONE

Documents from the Discussions with Leon Trotsky

I.

The 14 or 15 million Negroes in the U.S.A. represent potentially the most militant section of the population. Economic exploitation and the crudest forms of racial discrimination make this radicalization inevitable. We also have historical proof, first in the part played by the Negroes in the Civil War and in the response to a Marcus Garvey. Superficially, the Negro accepts, but that acceptance does not go very deep down. It is essentially dissimulation and a feeling of impotence, the age-old protective armor of the slave. It has been stated that the C.P. in organizing the Negroes in the South got such response that it had to check the campaign. The reason given was that owing to the number of Negroes joining and the fewness of the whites, the result would soon be a race-war between the Southern workers and sharecroppers.

II.

The Negro responds not only to national but international questions. It is stated that during the Ethiopian crisis, thousands of Negroes were ready to go to Ethiopia as fighters and nurses. Since the trouble in the West Indies, Jamaicans in New York have formed a Jamaica Progressive Association. They drafted a memorandum demanding a democratic constitution for the West Indies, sent a delegate to meet the Royal Commission and to visit Panama and Colon to organize membership of the association.

III.

Finally, I am informed that a new spirit is moving among the Negroes, in Harlem and elsewhere today. People who knew the Harlem Negro fifteen years ago and know him today state that the change is incredible. The Negro press today, poor as it is, is an immense advance on what it was five years ago. The *Pittsburgh Courier*, with a circulation of over 100,000 weekly, though a bourgeois paper, bitterly attacks the Roosevelt administration for its failure to deal with the Negro question. The younger generation in particular aims at equality, not to be discriminated against simply because they are black. To sum up then

(a) The Negro represents potentially the most revolutionary section of the population.

(b) He is ready to respond to militant leadership.

(c) He will respond to political situations abroad which concern him.

(d) He is today more militant than ever.

IV.

The Fourth International movement has neglected the Negro question almost completely. If even the Party personnel were not of a type to do active work among the Negro masses, the *Negro question* as an integral part of the American revolution can no longer be neglected. *The Negro helped materially to win the Civil War* and he can make the difference between success and failure in any given revolutionary situation. A Negro department of some sort should be organized (consisting, if need be, entirely of whites) which will deal as comprehensively with the Negro question as the Trade Union Department deals with the Trade Union Question. *If the Party thinks the question important enough this will be done.* The Party members and sympathizers must be educated to the significance of the Negro question. This is not a question of there being no Negroes in the Party. That has nothing to do with it at all. This work can begin immediately. The main question, however, that of organizing or helping to organize the Negro masses, is one of enormous difficulty for a party like the S.W.P. The main reasons for this are of course the discrimination against the Negro in industry by both capitalists and workers, the chauvinism of the white workers, and the political backwardness of the American movement. Each of these are fundamental causes inherent in the economic and social structure of the country.

But an already difficult situation has been complicated by the funereal role of the C.P., especially during the last few years. It is stated, and there is every reason to believe it, that the possibilities of a rapprochement between blacks and whites on a working class basis are today worse than they were ten years ago. The C.P. has lost 1,579 or 79% of its Negro membership during the last year in New York State alone. Since that time, there has taken place the split of the Workers Alliance, and New York is slated to be always symptomatic of developments in the Party as a whole. It was not always like this. I am informed that some years ago in Harlem, the Negro who was aware of politics might not join the C.P., but he would say that of all the white parties, the C.P. was the only party which did fight for Negro equality and which tried to stick to its principles. Today that is gone. The chief reason for this is, of course, the new Popular Front turn of the C.P. The C.P. cannot gain the allies it wants if it fights the difficult fight for Negro rights. The C.P. is now an American party, and the petty bourgeois supporters of democracy who are coming into it have nothing in common with the Negro, who, finding himself an outsider, has simply left the Party. I have had personal experience of the bitterness of ex-members of the C.P. toward the party, and unfortunately, to all white parties also.

But it is to be noted that the main grievance is political—the activity of the C.P. on the Ethiopian question. First of all, that Russia sold oil to Italy made a disastrous impression on the blacks. Yet many Negro party members remained. What seems to have been a decisive factor was the activity in regard to Spain and China and its lack of activity in regard to Ethiopia. "Every day it is only Spain, Spain, China, Spain, but nothing done for Ethiopia except one or two meager processions around Harlem." I have the impression that the C.P. could have gotten away with the Soviet selling of oil if it had carried on a vigorous campaign, collecting money, etc. for the Ethiopian cause. The contrast with Spain has been too glaring, and when the C.P. entirely neglected the West Indian situation, the Negroes became finally conscious that they were once more the dupes of "another white party."

The Ethiopian question and the West Indian question are still live questions for the politically minded Negroes. They will judge a Party on the international field by what it does or says on these issues.*

Articles, leaflets, and even small meetings in Harlem are not beyond the Party today with a little effort. One party comrade has managed to make himself familiar with the Indian problem, to write articles in the N.I, and to make valuable contacts. The same could surely be done nearer home.

France at the present time is the key to the world situation. How to awaken interest in the American Negroes on the critical situation in France, obviously of such importance to themselves? Obviously by the struggle for independence of the French colonies and particularly through the Negro organizations in Europe and Africa which are working towards this end. (The French party and with it the Belgian and British parties have their responsibility here.) In France today there are African revolutionary organizations in contact with a similar organization in Britain. The Fourth International must determinately assist in building and strengthening its connections with this work, and the American Party has its part to play in this important means of educating and organizing the Negro movement in America.

The most difficult question is still to be faced. What will the Party aim at in its Negro work? There are certain things that every revolutionary party will do:

(a) Fight for the Negroes' place and rights in the Trade Unions.

(b) Seek to make as many Negroes as possible members.

(c) Carry on a merciless struggle against White chauvinism.

About **(c)** a word should be said. The C.P. has been accused of fostering a black chauvinism. There have been exaggerations and absurdities and downright crimes against socialism, e.g. using white women to catch Negroes, but on the whole, the C.P. attitude of going to lengths in order to make the Negro feel that the C.P. looked upon him as a man and equal is not to be lightly dismissed. The general aim was correct. The Negro brought up in America or Africa is extremely sensitive to chauvinism of

---

* The neglect of the Ethiopian question by the Fourth International (the British Section included) is a grave strategic error. The Ethiopians are in the field fighting and are going to be there for years. If there is any break in Italy during a war, these fighters will sweep the isolated Italian force out of the country. The African revolution today has a starting point in Africa. It is obvious what effect any such sweeping victory by the Ethiopian army will have on French black troops in Western Europe, and on Africans.

any kind. Lenin knew this and in his thesis to the Second Congress on the Colonial Question, he warned that concessions would have to made to correct this justifiable suspicion on the part of the colonial workers. *No principled concession can ever be made.* But sensitiveness to "black chauvinism" will gain nothing and will do a great deal of harm. It should be noted that this suspicious attitude is not directed against whites only. Africans, and also to some degree Americans, are often hostile to educated West Indian Negroes who from their British education and the comparative absence of sharp racial discrimination in the West Indies are accused, and justly, of having a "superior" and "white" attitude. Organizations in London predominantly West Indian find it difficult to get African members, and in America, to get American members.

The party will base itself in the everyday needs of the Negroes. *It must aim at being a mass organization or it would be useless and mischievous.* The dangers of such an organization are obvious. But a recognition of these dangers does not solve two questions:

(1) The great masses of Negroes are unorganized and no white party is going to organize them. They will not join the Fourth International. Is it worthwhile to assist in the formation of an organization which will rally Negroes, and, though reformist in character, must from the very nature of its membership develop into a militant organization? The Negro has poured his money into Garvey's coffers, and now into Father Divine's, has worked hard and been robbed. Is there a way out for him to fight unless he joins the Fourth International?

(2) Though I may be wrong here, I think that such an organization is going to be formed whatever we do.

This question of the Negro organization is one that deserves the closest study. As far as I can see, no white leader or white organization is going to build a mass organization among the Negroes, either in Africa or in America. As recently as 1935, however, the Negroes have shown their capacity for mass political action under one of their own leaders. One, Sufi, a Southern Negro, masquerading as a man from the East, organized a party, picketed shops, and helped to force employers to give one-third of their jobs to Negroes. He was the leading figure in the riots which gained Harlem schools, more colored teachers, recreation grounds, etc. Sufi was a racketeering demagogue and was entangled into an Anti-Semitism which, I am informed, was no part of his creed, such as it was. But he was ready to fight for such things as the Negro understood and he got a strong response. The question, however, is pertinently asked: Why is it that intelligent Negroes with political understanding never attempt to lead Negroes but always leave them to men like Garvey and Sufi?

This, it seems to me, is one of the most important questions on which the party has to come to a decision. It is closely linked to the question of self-determination for American Negroes. Self-determination for the American Negroes is (1) economically reactionary and (2) politically false because no Negroes (except C.P. stooges) want it. For Negroes it is merely an inverted segregation. Yet it is not to be lightly dismissed without providing for what it aims at: the creation of confidence among the Negroes that revolutionary socialism does honestly and sincerely mean to stand by its promises. As so often with Marxists, the subsidiary psychological factors are not carefully provided for in the planning of political campaigns.

The Negro must be won for socialism. There is no other way out for him in America or elsewhere. But he must be won on the basis of his own experience and his own activity. There is no other way for him to learn, nor for that matter, for any other group of toilers. *If he wanted self-determination*, then however reactionary it might be in every other respect, it would be the business of the revolutionary party to raise that slogan. If after the revolution, he insisted on carrying out that slogan and forming his own Negro state, the revolutionary party would have to stand by its promises and (similarly to its treatment of large masses of the peasantry) patiently trust to economic development and education to achieve an integration. But the Negro, fortunately for Socialism, does not want self-determination.

Yet Negroes, individually and in the mass, will remain profoundly suspicious of whites. In private and in public, they ask the question: "How are we to know that after the revolution we shall not be treated in the same way?" Many who do not say this think it. The C.P. Negroes are looked upon as touts for Negro converts in exactly the same way as the Democratic and Republican Parties have touts for Negro votes. What is the remedy? *I propose that there is an obvious way—the organization of a Negro movement. That the Negro masses do certainly want—they will respond to that and therefore they must have it.* They will follow such a movement ably and honestly led. They have followed similar movements in the past *and are looking for a similar movement now*.

The great argument for such a movement is that it has the possibility of setting the Negro masses in motion, the only way in which they will learn the realities of political activity and be brought to realize the necessity of mortal struggle against capitalism. Who opposes such a procedure must have some concrete suggestions for attaining this most important end: bringing Negro masses into the struggle.

What precise aims will such an organization have? What it must not at any cost do is to seek to duplicate existing white organizations so as to result in anything like dual unionism, etc. One of its main tasks will be to demand and struggle for *the right of the Negro to full participation in all industries and in all unions*. Any Negro organization which fought militantly for such an aim would thereby justify its existence.

There are many urgent issues: the struggle for the Negro right to vote, against social and legal discrimination, against discrimination in schools (and universities), against oppressive rents. The struggle against such things and the task of bringing the white workers to see to a concrete realization of their responsibility in these questions can be best achieved by a combination of the few politically advanced whites *backed by a powerful Negro movement*. To expect a continuous struggle by the whites on these Negro issues is absurd to lay down as a condition. For what it amounts to—that the Negro cannot struggle against these things unless he forms organizations predominantly white—is sectarian and stupid.

The Negro himself will have the satisfaction of supporting his own movement. The constant domination of whites, whether by the bourgeoisie or in workers' movements, more and more irks the Negro. That is why he followed a Marcus Garvey in such hundreds of thousands and would not join the C.P. The Party's attitude towards such a movement should therefore be one of frank, sincere, and unwavering support. The white proletariat will have to demonstrate concretely its value to the Negro not once, but many times, before it wins the Negro's confidence.

The support of this movement by the Party should be frank, sincere, and unwavering. This is not as easy as it sounds. What the Party must avoid at all costs is looking upon such a movement as a recruiting ground for party members, something to be "captured" or manipulated for the aims of the party, or something which it supports spasmodically at the time it needs something in return. The party should frankly and openly endorse such a movement, urge Negroes to join it, assist the movement in every way and, while pointing out the political differences and showing that revolutionary socialism is the ultimate road, work side by side to influence this movement by criticism and activity combined. It is in this way and on the basis of a common struggle, with the party always helping by never seeking to manipulate the movement, that the confidence of the Negro movement be gained by revolutionary socialism, without raising the impracticable slogan of self-determination.

What are the dangers of such a movement? The chief are: **(a)** the danger that it might be used by reactionary elements such as the Democratic Party or the Communist Party, **(b)** the danger of encouraging racial chauvinism. A fortunate combination of circumstances reduces these dangers to manageable proportions.

At the present moment, there is a sufficient number of capable Negroes ready and willing to lead such a movement who, while willing to cooperate with white parties, have no racial chauvinism.

While all Negroes will be admitted and racial discrimination against any Negro as a Negro will be fought, it is recognized by all with whom I have discussed this question, that such a movement must be a mass movement based on the demands of Negro workers and peasants. Much will depend on the leadership here. I see no reason, however, to have any doubts on this score. Such a leadership exists at the present time and needs only be mobilized. The Negro's right to his place in industry and the trade unions must be one of the main planks of the platform and one of the main fields of activity. The prospective leadership, as I see it, will be militantly opposed to the political line and organizational practice of the C.P.

Yet this is not sufficient as a political basis. Sooner or later the organization will have to face its attitude towards capitalism. Is it to be a reformist or revolutionary organization? It will not start as a full-fledged revolutionary socialist organization. As Lenin pointed out to the pioneers of communism in Britain immediately after the war, it would be a mistake to flaunt the banner of revolution right at the beginning. *The basis of the organization must be the struggle for the day-to-day demands of the Negro.* But the American economy is already and will increasingly pose the question to every political organization—fascism or communism. Here again the initial leadership will exercise a decisive influence. This is a question which will ultimately be decided by struggle within the organization.

However, many factors are in favor of a victory ultimately for those who support revolutionary socialism, when the Negro masses are ready for it. First there is the question of revolutionary struggle for the Negroes in Africa against imperialism. On this, most politically minded Negroes are agreed. Secondly, the International African Service Bureau, a British organization, issued a Manifesto during the Munich crisis which demands a joint struggle of British workers in Britain and colonials of the Empire for the overthrow of Imperialism. This Manifesto has been warmly welcomed among advanced Negroes in America, and the bureau and its paper, *International African Opinion*, have already a powerful influence, and this not only on account of its policy, but because it is run by Negroes.

Militant struggle for day-to-day demands must be the basis and constant activity of the movement, but in this period, action on this basis will drive the movement sharply up against the capitalist state and fascists or neo-fascist bands; and the transition to revolutionary socialism will not ultimately be difficult. As soon as this organization has achieved a firm basis, an international conference will most probably be called between the various militant Negro organizations and from my personal knowledge of them and their personnel, there is a probability that Socialism may be adopted. Such are the possibilities at the present time. And it is fortunate that they are so favorable. *But it must be insisted upon that support of a Negro mass movement must not be conditional upon whether it is or soon will be socialist or not.* It is the awakening and bringing into political activity of the large mass of Negroes which is the main consideration, and to this the party must give its frank, sincere, and unwavering support. The rest depends on the development of the whole international situation, the struggle of revolutionary parties, e.g. the growth of the S.W.P. and the individuals who will constitute the leadership.

On the specific danger of racial chauvinism, I shall say little; in my view, it is for the movement of the kind projected a minor question. No movement which proclaims the Negro's right to his place in the trade unions can be deeply penetrated with chauvinism. The Negroes who are likely to lead this movement see the dangers of chauvinism as clearly as the whites do. In America, where the Negroes are in a definite minority, serious fear of black chauvinism on the part of white revolutionaries seems to me not only unnecessary but dangerous. In the concrete instance, black chauvinism is a progressive force, it is the expression of a desire for equality of an oppressed and deeply humiliated people. The persistent refusal to have "self-determination" is evidence of the limitation of black chauvinism in America. Any excessive sensitiveness to black chauvinism by the white revolutionaries is the surest way to create hostilities and suspicion among the black people.

Such, in outline, it seems to me, should be the attitude of the party towards such an organization. It should actively assist the formation of such a movement. In any case, I have little doubt that such a movement is going to be formed sooner or later. But the party also has its own responsibility to the Negro question. The following are a few observations, based on a necessarily limited knowledge of the American situation, learned chiefly by discussion with Negro Socialists or near-Socialists.

(a) Earlier I stated that the Party must form a section devoted entirely to the Negro question. This is urgent work, whether a Negro organization is formed or not. Our great weapon at the present moment is Marxism by which we illuminate every grave social and political problem of the day. The Party's first task, therefore, is to do what no organization, white or Negro, can do completely unless it is based on the principles of Marxism, study the Negro question in relation to the national and international situation.

(b) The Negro Committee should embark on an unremitting study of the Negro question, and immediately make arrangements for the publication of articles regularly in the *Socialist Appeal* and the *New International*. The *Appeal* should have a weekly column devoted to the Negro question. It will not be difficult to get regular information if contact is kept with Negroes. Not only accounts of lynchings, specific discriminations in industry, etc., but the presentation and analysis of various economic and social statistics issued, with special reference to the Negro, the colonial struggle in Africa, etc. This must now be a prominent and permanent section of the party's work, for Party members as well as Negro contacts.

Particularly urgent for the *New International* is an article or series of articles written from the inside and exposing the dealings of the American Communist Party with the Negro. The political line, the activities of Ford, Richard Moore, and Co., would be shown up, and their political corruption and degeneration traced in relation to the decline of the Comintern. The Negroes must be shown why the C.P. policy to the Negro has been what it has been at different times and why. The bureaucratic "promotion" and "demotion" of Negroes must be shown as a direct reflection of the bureaucratic degeneration of the Russian Revolution. A series of articles and a pamphlet relating the C.P. political and organizational policy towards Negroes with the zigzags of the Comintern would be of inestimable value. This should be done as a first task.

(c) The numerous Negro organizations in Harlem and elsewhere must be contacted. This should be done very carefully, for the C.P. policy of "penetration" or "capturing from within" and generally of being concerned chiefly with bringing the organization under its influence, *and not with helping in the Negro struggle*, has borne bitter fruit, and the attitude towards any white is likely to be "What have you come here to get?" That the party should encourage the formation of a Negro mass movement does not mean that it will in any way cease activity to gain membership among Negroes. What is to be avoided is the impression that it is interested in Negro activity solely for the purpose of getting members or influence, and not for the purpose of assisting Negro struggles. That would be a grave crime not only against Negroes but against the socialist movement. Yet the party will openly and frankly seek membership. It seems, however, that here certain dangers are to be avoided.

The NAACP, the Urban League, and other Negro organizations, weekly forums, etc., carry on a certain amount of activity. Mere condemnation of these as bourgeois is worse than useless. *At present*, in most areas, the party's appeal to most Negroes would chiefly be to those who are attracted by its superior understanding and analysis of the Negro question and the world situation. But these Negroes, when won, must not be immediately abstracted from their milieu and plunged into the struggle against Stalinism, etc. One of their main tasks at the present stage is to remain among the Negroes in their areas in the local organizations, carrying on an active fight for the party's ideas in a manner carefully adapted to their hearers' point of view. Broadly speaking, among whites there is a differentiation; revolutionaries circle around revolutionary organizations, and the petty bourgeois democrats belong to the various petty bourgeois organizations. Among Negroes, especially in the provinces, it is not so. All types, instinctive revolutionaries and conservatives, can be found at the local Negro forums, Y.M.C.A. etc. even though these meetings often begin with prayers. There is a vast field here for the winning of Negro members to the party *if the party press and literature give them a weapon which they can use.*

But at the same time, the party must beware of looking upon Negro work as to be done necessarily by Negroes. The clearance of the long road to socialist equality must begin at once. Certain white comrades can now begin to become experts on the Negro question. The method is easy to define, hard to carry out. It means a regular reading of the Negro press, Negro literature, regular attendance at Negro meetings, etc. The arguments for socialism are to be directed against the latest pronouncements of Kelly, Miller, Mordecai, Johnson, George, Schulyer, the local Negro representatives of the Republican and Democratic parties, not against Stalin, Daladiuer, and Chiang Kai-Sheck. And to attempt to do propaganda among Negroes on any other basis than attack, debate, exposition, etc. concerned with the writers, press etc. read by the Negroes, is to speak a language alien to them. This is of particular importance in areas where the Party is small. (For the moment I exclude organizations of the Negro unemployed etc. which would more properly be the problem of the Trade Union Section). A close attention by one or two white comrades to the discussion, literature, etc. of the various Negro groups in their community must bear fruit in the end owing to the superior power of the ideas we put forward. And while Negroes will do the main part of this work, even where the Party has Negro comrades, white comrades must take their part and will win great prestige for the party by showing themselves thoroughly familiar with Negro life and thought. We must work patiently in the rather restricted milieu to which even groups of educated Negroes are condemned by their position in American society.

The Committee should get into contact with the French, British, Belgian, and South African sections, get regular information about their work and contacts, a good supply of British and South African papers, especially those dealing with colonial questions, and circulate these and translations from the French among the Negro organizations and interested groups and persons. Every effort should be made to circulate the *Spark* widely among interested Negro contacts. The International African Service Bureau and its organ, *International African Opinion*, should be popularized by the party among Negroes and whites alike. Negroes will welcome and appreciate this. This organization of Fourth International colonial activity in a manner to present it constantly and regularly to Negroes in America, is not only one of the most important means of drawing Negro contact ultimately into our party. It means also, and this is of immense importance in our period, that Negro organizations everywhere which are internationally minded or drawing towards internationalism will ultimately realize that the only genuine international organization in the world at the present time is the Fourth International.

Notes Following the Discussions (1939)

In *The New Negro* by Alain Locke there is a reference to the fact that Garvey preached an exclusively black doctrine of race—only Negroes who were black were truly Negroes. This statement is of the first importance.

In America today, there are caste divisions among the blacks themselves and these are based on color. They are most clearly seen in the church. The mulattoes are petty bourgeois members of the Roman Catholic and Episcopalian (orthodox Protestant) churches. The blacks, the poorest, the most oppressed, are members of the Baptist and African Methodist Churches, the great stronghold of the black parsons and to this day the most powerful national organizations created and controlled entirely by Negroes.

It was on this stratum that Garvey built his movement; his appeal to the "pure" black shows that. Also, they had just emigrated and were still coming in hundreds of thousands from the South, a proletarian and sub-proletarian mass getting better wages for the first time and rising to the possibilities that even the limited freedom of the North allowed them.

I have personal experience of these people, particularly in an "Ethiopian" movement in New York and in one of the "black" churches which I attended. The "Ethiopians" are fanatically chauvinistic and on the night I spoke to them two white comrades evoked great hostility. But of their revolutionary ardor there was no doubt. A similar passion was also obvious in the church service, and there, the weeping, the shaking of hands, the response to the preacher's references to oppression, were no doubt a sublimation of revolutionary emotion. The greatest response was made to the passage on oppression and suffering.* Garvey raised these people to political activity. His movement fell, and today their leader is Father Divine, merely a super-preacher and demagogue combined.

But the great response to **(a)** Freedom in Africa, **(b)** Freedom in Ethiopia, **(c)** Freedom in Heaven, seems to point to the fact that self-determination, i.e. a black state in the South would awaken a response among these masses, as bitterly as it is opposed by all the intellectuals and more literate among the Negroes. This is the *tentative* conclusion I have come to after carefully considering the course of our discussion and thinking back over the contacts I made with this stratum during my short stay in America. This of course will have to be tested by experience, but another question arises.

If it does prove to be so, the slogan of a "black state" will come badly from the S.W.P. It will infallibly awaken great suspicion among the Negroes.

---

* This clergyman offered me his pulpit for a Sunday evening—an audience of 800 people, the poorest of the poor. I could not do so before I left New York, but I asked him to wait until I returned. I shall make a cautious but clear appeal for revolutionary action and particularly raise the question of a black state.

"They want to get rid of us." Coming, however, from Negro intellectuals in a Negro movement, if there is the latent response, it will be accepted without difficulty. The S.W.P. can then support it wholeheartedly.

The success of the Garvey movement, of the Divine movement, and the millions of dollars poor Negroes pour annually into the churches out of their almost empty purses, all these are evidence of their fanatical devotion and capacity for self-sacrifice. And the revolutionary energy, the readiness to give all which distinguished the Garvey movement in particular, in return for nothing tangible but the promise of a new society, show that here, in contradistinction to the great movements of organized workers for higher wages, closed shop, etc., we have perhaps the most important manifestation in American capitalist society of one most powerful current in the coming socialist revolution. The party must find a way to these millions and I am more than ever convinced that the way is through a Negro organization, going over the literate and vocal intellectuals and finding the masses whom Garvey found.

TWO

Pages from an Organizer's Notebook

If We Must Die

If we must die—let it not be like hogs
Hunted and penned in an inglorious spot,
While round us bark the mad and hungry dogs,
Making their mock at our accursed lot.

If we must die—oh, let us nobly die,
So that our precious blood may not be shed
In vain; then even the monsters we defy
Shall be constrained to honor us though dead!

Oh, Kinsmen! We must meet the common foe;
Though far outnumbered, let us still be brave,
And for their thousand blows deal one death blow!
What though before us lies the open grave?
Like men we'll face the murderous, cowardly pack,
Pressed to the wall, dying, but fighting back!

—Claude McKay

My Friends:

  In this moment of crisis, it is proper that the voice of the working man should be heard. The President governs for all, the priests pray for all, the soldier fight for all (so, at any rate, we are told) but it is the working man who pays for all. In times of peace he pays in labor and in sweat. In war be pays in blood. It is always the working man and the farmers who are placed in the front line trenches. The sons of the rich stay behind the lines and direct. I have been to war and I know.

  That is why I claim the privilege of a broadcast. I am a black working man, but I am a native son, as American as any white man in this country. My people were here as early as the family of President Roosevelt. We Negroes have labored and helped to make this country what it is. We have fought in all its wars, from the War of Independence to the first World War. In fact Crispus Attucks, a Negro, was the first American to die in the American Revolution. So that when the President talks about preparing America for war I demand my right to be heard. I know how to make a fireside chat. You are all sitting down listening to me and I am sitting down talking to you. You know it, I know it, everybody knows it. But in order to make you feel that you will be getting the real inside dope in a confidential manner, I shall begin by saying: "My friends, let us sit down, you and I, and talk this thing over together." That piece of baloney being out of the way, we can now get down to business.

Is America in Danger?

The President says that Hitler seems to be winning the European war, and for that reason, this country is in danger of being invaded. Maybe the country is really in danger. But from the start this whole invasion business seemed phony to me. I went to France in the last war, and I saw what it takes to carry a million men across the Atlantic and to keep them there. Germany is very near to England. Yet everybody says that Hitler had to capture Normandy and the Channel ports and get within a few miles of England in order to attempt a successful invasion. Who is such a fool as to believe that Hitler can transport millions of men and all the arms and supplies needed to invade this country, across nearly 3,000 miles of sea? The Yankee Clipper takes only 20 passengers at a time. How many clippers will Hitler need to land a million men in America? Hitler would have to spend years in preparation before he could invade this country. Furthermore, the Presidents knows that all this talk about invasion is just a lot of hooey. My wife Leonora, who is a Red, told me that the other day the generals of the army and navy made an official statement that this country was in no danger of invasion. And if they know that, and I know it, the President knows it too.

When I said to some of my friends, poor trembling Negroes, that they had many things to worry about but that invasion is not one of them, they asked me, "But do you think that the President is lying? Why should he lie? He only wants to protect the people." My friends, and particularly my young friends, let me show you how a President can lie. I went to hear President Wilson speak in 1916. He said that we must vote for him because he was the man who had kept us out of war. And as soon as he had won the elections he carried out the plan he had in his pocket for almost a year before the elections, and we were in the war before you could wink. Since that time, my friends, I know how Presidents can lie. Wilson wanted to get us in and he used one jive. Roosevelt wants to get us in and he is using another one. He wants to frighten us with the fear of invasion, although his own generals and admirals tell us the exact opposite.

Defend What Democracy?

My friends, why does the President want us to fight? He and all the writers in the papers say that it is to defend our democracy. Our democracy! My friends, when I heard that I laughed for ten minutes. Yes. Laughed. I'll tell you why. It was because I was so damned mad that if I didn't laugh I would have broken the radio. And that radio cost me $4 in the pawn shop and I didn't want to break it.

Tell me, Mr. President, what democracy do I defend by going to fight Hitler? Hitler is a vile criminal and should be driven off the face of the earth. But I have no democracy and the democracy I haven't got Hitler didn't take from me. I know all those who have been taking away democracy from me and my people. They are Cotton Ed Smith, Senator Bilbo, Vice President Garner, all of them aided by you, President Roosevelt, for all of you are in one Party together, the Democratic Party, and if you were any friend of the Negro, you couldn't be working so closely in the same Party with those Negro-hating, Negro-baiting little American Hitlers from the South. William Green, president of the American Federation of Labor, who discriminates against Negroes in his unions is another. There are thousands of others I could name. They have been lynching me and my people, giving us the dirtiest jobs, at the lowest pay, Jim Crowing us, taking the taxes we pay to teach white children, treating us worse than they treat their dogs. They were doing all this before Hitler was born, they are doing it now, they will do it long after Hitler is dead, unless we Negroes ourselves put a stop to it. I never heard any fireside chat from you, Mr. President, I never saw any campaign carried out by the Senate, to give the American Negroes democracy—for instance, to pass the anti-lynching bill or abolish Jim Crow and the poll tax, which prevents Negroes in the South from voting. May I tell you Mr. President, politely as suits a fireside chat, that you and the hypocritical scoundrels who rule this country with you, should stop being so active in defense of democracy abroad and pay attention to the crimes against democracy at home. Instead, your newspapers spread a lot of lies about no lynchings having taken place during the past year. As if they don't know that nowadays the Southern lynchers get together in small bands and murder any Negro whom they want to get rid of, very quietly so as to keep it out of the papers.

The Fifth Column

My friends, the President warns us about the fifth column. I understand that this is the new name for the enemies of democracy. Where have the President's eyes been all this time? If he wants to find out who these fifth column people are, he just has to ask the Negroes. We know them. We spend our lives fighting against them. If the President sends a reporter to me, with a large notebook, I guarantee that between sunrise and sundown tomorrow I'll point out to him more fifth column enemies of democracy than he can find room for in all the jails of this country. No, Mr. President, we'll begin to listen to you about the fifth column when you begin to put in jail some of the really big enemies of democracy in this country, beginning with the United States Vice President, Jack Garner, boss of the Jim Crow state of Texas.

My friends, the President and all the papers say that we must stop aggression. But when Mussolini made his aggression against Ethiopia, you, Mr. President, prevented us from sending arms to Ethiopia. Where was all your hatred of aggression then? But I notice that today you have the American fleet ready to fight Japan for the Dutch East Indies. My wife Leonora, who is a Red, tells me that America wants to fight Germany to prevent Hitler taking the colonies of the Allied countries, and to keep Germany as much as possible out of the fat trade with China and Spanish America. That makes sense to me. But what I know is this, that whatever

President Roosevelt wants to fight about, it is not democracy. I have no interests in the Dutch East Indies. The natives there got no democracy from the Dutch. They will get no democracy from America. They will get none from Japan. They will get some democracy only when they drive out all these leeches and take charge of their country themselves.

Democracy Begins at Home

My friends, it is not only the poor Negroes who get no democracy. The other day I saw a picture, *The Grapes of Wrath*. In it I saw whites, miserable and suffering almost as much as we Negroes suffer. Every week outside the relief station there are whites standing with me, no better off than I am. If these poor Okies and the Negroes and the white workers were to get together we could fight for some real democracy here. That is the fight I am willing to begin. I know who my enemies are. And when these same enemies come telling me about going to fight against Hitler, what I tell them in my mind is what would be very out of place in a fireside chat, so you will have to guess at it.

I know a Negro school teacher who says that we must fight with Roosevelt to defeat Hitler. I want to see Hitler defeated but why should I trust Roosevelt? How do I know that Roosevelt at some time or another wouldn't turn traitor? Look at the King of Belgium. He must have told the poor Belgians to come and fight with him for democracy. Now he has surrendered to Hitler and next thing he will be helping Hitler to impose fascism on the Belgian people. That is what you get when you listen to these Kings and Presidents and Generals all urging poor people to come and fight against Hitler. I have been watching that school teacher a long time. And I think that what he wants to defend is not democracy but the $35 a week he gets for teaching in the Jim Crow school. If he want to die for democracy and his $35, that is his business. But he isn't going to lead me into that. When he have defeated the enemies of democracy here, then we can give Hitler a beating. I would be ready to fight against Hitler then.

Unite and Fight!

My friends, Negroes are well known for their belief in God. And I notice that a good fireside chat always has something in it about God and prayers. But I notice too that Hitler in all his speeches talks about God and asks for his blessing. President Wilson, that smooth-tongued rascal, was full of God too. But Roosevelt, Hitler, and Wilson not only pray to God, but see to it that they have guns, battleship, and planes. So tonight, my friends, my dear friends, I want to leave out the prayers and tell you plainly what is my policy for the American people and the Negroes in particular. It is this. Unite and fight for our democracy here. What I as a black man want is a steady job. I want good wages, $30 a week for 30 hours a week. I want a good relief check when I am out of work. I want my black children to go to any school in the neighborhood. I want a good house and I want it where I choose to have it. I want to travel where I want, go where I want, eat where I want, join any union or organization that I want. I want this for myself, I want it for all my black people, and if any white man is prepared to join with us to fight for that, I want it for him too. And it isn't Hitler who is keeping these things from me. It is those who are robbing, cheating, and insulting my people.

My friends, to win those things I am prepared to fight. I may go to jail in that fight. I may get shot down by the police but I'll die contented. Death is death and I prefer to die fighting here for my rights and the rights of my people and those who will fight with us, than die so that President Roosevelt and his friends might get the Dutch East Indies or the British West Indies or any kind of Indies whatsoever. So, my friends, good night. I shall not quote scripture but I shall end with a piece of personal history. I went to the last war. I was treated like a dog before I went. I was treated like a dog while I was there. I was treated like a dog when I returned. I have been played for a sucker before, and I am not going to be played again.

WITH THE SHARECROPPERS (1941)

Among the one-third of the nation that lives in direst poverty and greatest misery are thousands upon thousands of sharecroppers, Negro and white, in Arkansas, Missouri, and other states. Ill housed, ill-clad, ill-fed, they daily feel the severest lash of landlord and government. But, despite the most vicious exploitation, despite terror—yes, actual, real terror—and despite starkest oppression, these are men whose spirits have not been broken, who stand ready to fight with every worker against class tyranny. They hunger for bread and they hunger for freedom. And, a fighting militant as every one of them is, they mean to satisfy these hungers, however great the odds against them, however dangerous the battle. They know their enemies and they will not yield.

I.

In 1934 the Roosevelt Administration passed the Agricultural Adjustment
Act to help the farmers. It aimed at cutting down the acreage of cotton by
one-third. For such is capitalism that cotton is plowed under while millions
go naked. Country committees were to work out the details based on an
average of five years previous. The government set an arbitrary price of
11 or 12 cents and paid the farmer the difference between that and what
he got on the open market. The surplus, millions of bales, was stacked
in government warehouses. (The Roosevelt Administration probably sees
some way of using it now in making bandages for the war.) To enrich the
soil one third of the crop was to be plowed under and soil conservation
payments were made to the landlord, providing that the money advanced
by the government should be shared by the farmer. On paper it was
beautiful.

To prevent cheating by the landlord, the law provided that the landlord
could not make any change in his condition of ownership, etc. But the
landlord is himself the law. He evaded this by making a bogus sale to
his brother or a friend and fixed things up to suit himself. The county
committees are landowners themselves or friends of landowners. They sign
statements proving that the conditions were always as they wanted them
arranged, in order to pocket as much of the government's subsidy as possible
and leave the poorer farmers and "croppers" starving as before.

By 1938 the landlord calculated that if he had no tenant farmers and
no sharecroppers he would not have to divide the government's subsidy
with anybody. The sharecropper's contract is from January to December,
and in January 1939 the landlords in southeast Missouri gave notice to the
sharecroppers to vacate by January 10. Twenty thousand workers were told
to leave the shacks in which they lived. They had nowhere to go. Some
of them scattered and sought refuge with a brother here or a cousin there
or a friend somewhere else. Where a two-room shack had housed four
persons, it now housed six. Families broke up. But 1,500 families, about
5,000 people, Negroes for the most part, with a few whites, camped on
the St. Louis highway. They took their scanty possessions with them and
announced their intention of staying there until the government took some
steps on their behalf.

It is true that this was a lock-out far more than it was a strike. But the
action itself was no spontaneous protest springing from a sudden emergency

(though it would have been none the less significant). As far back as 1935, Braxton Taylor, a Negro sharecropper of Texas bend, finding conditions unbearable, wrote a letter to an official of the Socialist Party of Missouri asking for help. He wrote to this address because he had seen the name in *The Call*, the Socialist Party newspaper.

A few months before, the Southern Tenant Farmers Union had been formed in Terrel, Arkansas. After some months a unit was formed in southeast Missouri. There were no organizers, but sharecroppers and day hands heard of the new organization through a grapevine and joined.

In Arkansas there was vicious oppression of the union and long battles. There were no strikes, no collective action. The frame of the union remained, however, and late in 1938 a Mr. Whitfield, a preacher, began to go round organizing. A local landowner wrote some articles sympathetic to the cause in the *St. Louis Post-Dispatch*. Whitfield, in an automobile, visited locals and agitated. A natural leader, fluent from his practice in the pulpit, and a man who had worked in the field as a day hand himself, he could speak from experience. Late in December he was speaking to meetings that overflowed church houses. The socialists who had helped to organize the local in the first place assisted in the organization. It was in this way that the roadside demonstration was prepared. A *Post-Dispatch* reporter, who heard about the coming action three days before it was due, gave the news away. But neither the reporter himself nor the landlords believed that the sharecroppers had spine enough to carry out the threat.

However, the walkout was a complete success. People flocked down and took up positions in three groups by the roadside. They were members of the Southern Tenant Farmers Union, so they called on the union for assistance. Butler, the leader of the STFU replied to Whitfield: "You did it without consulting us. Go back." The St. Louis Urban League and the CIO organized assistance and sent food. But the Stalinists in the CIO demanded as a condition that the strikers enter the United Cannery, Agricultural, Packing, and Allied Workers of America (UCAPAWA). Whitfield agreed.

There are many aspects to what happened on the roadside and a full account must be written some day, because it is a landmark in the history of the class struggle in America. Police, armed to the teeth, came to intimidate these Negroes and make them leave the highway. The Negroes, who had their guns with them, resolutely refused. The Health Department and the Humane Society came out and investigated. The sit-down strike was called a menace to public health. The chief of police and other officials came to get the strikers to move on. The result was nil. There they were and there they were going to stay.

It was bitterly cold and they lived in tents or in the open and babies were born on the highway. At last, by a trick, the police got hold of the strikers' guns and they were forced to go back to the Spillway. This is land lower than the river, which in the event of an overflow becomes flooded. It is damp and marshy. Here, at any rate, they were out of sight of the public.

About two weeks later they had to give in. They were shepherded away into livery stables, schools, broken down public buildings, and holes and hovels of all kinds. A very small percentage of the landlords took croppers back, and some were lured back to the cottages on the promise that they would not be charged any rent. On July 1, however, eviction notices were served on them and some went to jail The majority lived how they could, but most of them went back to work as day laborers. As such they had no interest or concern with any payments made to the landlord, according to the Agricultural Adjustment Act.

Some liberals in St. Louis formed a rehabilitation committee and about a hundred miles away they found a piece of land, infertile and rocky, and at the top of a hill. It was situated in the county of New Madrid, Miss. Three hundred and five families made the trek to it, and they began life over on July 3, 1939.

Just like pilgrims who had landed in America 300 years before, they set to work with axes and shovels, building log cabins and dirt floors. About a thousand people lived on bread and gravy for two months, bread made of flour, water, and salt. The local relief committee gave them as little as possible, hoping to throw them out. The sheriff threatened them. "You must not stay here. Tonight I will protect you, but after that I can't." However, they stayed at the camp, Poplar Bluff, and they built a village which they still inhabit. Of the three hundred and five families who went, five were white.

The action itself has had a tremendous moral effect on the Negroes themselves, on the landlords, and on the government. The situation in southeast Missouri can never be the same again. We shall later trace in detail what has been the result upon the workers. For the moment it will be sufficient to show what is now the attitude of the government. Late in 1939 the Negroes began to threaten to hold another roadside demonstration. The governor of Missouri was running for senator and he feared the adverse publicity. Through Bishop Scarlett of the Episcopal Church and one or two other liberals, he got in touch with a St. Louis socialist who he knew had influence among the sharecroppers. Whitfield, president of the union, was on a Stalinist tour and was summoned back immediately.

Meanwhile, John Moore, area president, was summoned to the governor's presence. The governor put his cards on the table. He had heard that there was another roadside demonstration projected. He could settle all difficulties. He would give every landless farmer a house and land if Moore called the demonstration off. The governor himself, the head of the state police, the head of the WPA, the head of the local relief administration, the head of the State Social Security Board, and four policemen—all in the room at the same time—met Moore and tried to beat him down. The governor promised 10,000 houses in 20 days and ten acres of land for each family. Moore, supported by his socialist friends, refused to commit the union. He could do nothing, he said, without the union. Having failed with Moore, the governor got hold of Whitfield at the Park Plaza Hotel, having paid all this expenses back from his tour, with cigars included.

Where Moore had held firm, Whitfield capitulated and agreed to call off the projected demonstration. Today the government has built 500 instead of 10,000 houses and instead of ten acres of land, each house has three-quarters of an acre allotted to it.

II.

We must get some clear idea of the type of workers who made the demonstrations, and what they have developed into.

These southeast Missouri Negroes are unique. All the statistics of the Bureau of Commerce will be useless unless we understand what type of people they are and the conditions which have shaped them.

Let us begin with one characteristic cropper. He is in the early thirties and was born in Mississippi. He went 2 1/2 miles to school every day and left in the fourth grade. He can read. He is also familiar with automobiles and machinery. He is no pro-war monger. At 14 he came to southeast Missouri. He first worked in the cotton field plowing behind a team. That was in 1924. He got $1.25 a day, from March until April 30. How many hours a day did he work? The answer is concise: "All."

In June the cotton chopping began. Again he got $1.25 a day. This lasted until the middle of July. There was no more work until the last week in September, when the picking started. This was piece work. Every 100 pounds, 75 cents. Some strong fellows picked 200 or even 250 pounds. The average man picked 150 pounds. The women would pick about 100 pounds. This stopped in December and there was no more work until the next March.

He lived in an old shack. When it rained he couldn't sleep, for the water came in, summer and winter. This was his life from 1923 to 1937.

In 1935 he heard of the NAACP through the local preacher. He joined. There were about 100 members in his local. In 1938 he heard of the union for the first time. As soon as he heard of it he joined. Whitfield came to speak to a meeting and there were 150 present. In 1939 he took part in the demonstration, was one of the leaders.

After the demonstration he went back to work. This time he and his family lived with two other families in three rooms. The pay was $1.00 a day. The landlord was using tractors, not horses. He needed labor only for chopping cotton and picking. Where one man used to do 10 acres a day, the tractor does 33.

He and his wife made a crop in 1938. They farmed 11 acres. Starting January 1 they got $12 a month for five months. The landlord furnished mule and plow and fed the livestock. In September they started to pick. The price of cotton was 10 to 10 1/2 cents. The landlord paid him 8 1/2 to 9 cents. He made nine bales at 500 pounds a bale. The total amount was $405. His share was therefore $202.50 minus an advance of $60 and other minor advances.

However, in December when he was paid off he got $4.55. Parity payment he got none of, because the landlord, before paying off the crop, insisted that the parity payment be turned over to him. If one were writing fiction it would be necessary to change $4.55, to make it a little more reasonable in appearance. In fact, the actual truth is worse. The cropper's brother was making a crop of 11 acres for the same landlord. In June he got a job on the WPA at $8 a week and left the crop. The cropper took it over and made nine bales of cotton. The $4.55 he received was for both crops.

In another area one hundred miles off, it was stated that the croppers got what was due to them. The practice of stealing by the landlords varies from state to state and district to district. But there is scarcely a Negro in the area who does not know that he must work a few months of the year, all the hours of the day, for $1.25 a day (when it does not rain) or do share-cropping and be at the complete mercy of the landlord.

The recent case where a landlord shot a cropper dead because he dared to argue with him is no ordinary murder. It typifies the economic relation between ruler and worker in the process of production.

This was the experience behind the demonstration. And it would be a grave mistake to underestimate it. Three generations of Negroes have suffered it and they have had enough. Today the Negroes in southeast Missouri wish neither to be day laborers nor sharecroppers. They have had their fill of both.

Even in those areas where the croppers admitted that they got their share, they do not want to be sharecroppers any more. Share or no share, the economic and social conditions are such as to create a permanent poverty, misery, and degradation which have made thousands of them ready for anything. There are about 20,000 day laborers in this part of the state and about 5,000 took part in the demonstration. Its importance is that it is the first attempt at mass action to remedy an intolerable situation.

The proportion is very high. Everything now starts from the demonstration. They think in terms of it. A careful account of it should be written, the good points emphasized and the mistakes and weaknesses pointed out. The action has given them a sense of power and a consciousness of solidarity.

Naturally with their dispersal and the passing of time, this cohesion may seem to have been dissipated. It is not so. It is there, as can be seen from conversations with any half dozen separate individuals. It forms a practical and psychological basis for the organization of the sharecroppers to take industrial and political action. The masses learn best from the examination and analysis of their own common experience.

The more farsighted of them know what the demonstration has done for them. There were actual concrete results. Just before it took place certain landlords were plotting together to change the proportion in which the crop was divided and rob the cropper some more. In the present system the cropper gets one-half of the crop. The landlord, who actually owns the land, gets one quarter and the entrepreneur, who rented from the landlord, gets the other quarter. The new scheme that was being hatched aimed at giving the landlord one-quarter of the crop. That left three quarters, which was to be divided between the entrepreneur and the sharecropper, each getting three-eighths. Thus the sharecropper would lost one-eight of his previous share. But when the demonstration took place landlords and entrepreneurs retreated.

No working class or section of the working class hates the ruling class as these sharecroppers hate their rulers. They know that the main enemy is at home. They can see it. The enemy is not a trust, nor a corporation, nor figures in a bank. He is there, visible. The burden of the sharecropper's complaint is that the landlord sits in his house, does nothing, and gets everything, while they do all the work and get nothing.

There is Walter Richardson, for instance, owner of a cotton gin and landowner, who says that no "niggers" will get any payments from him and, left to him, he would run every Negro out of southeast Missouri. The croppers state that they have put him where he is, and this is the way that he is talking about them now.

There is J. B. Conrad, prosecuting attorney of New Madrid County, who makes it known that no Negro is to come to him to prosecute any white man.

There is P. M. Barton with 55,000 acres, who employs 5,000 day laborers and sharecroppers. He is a millionaire many times over and the contrast between his wealth and their misery is too much for the Negro worker.

The experience of generations has taught them that there is no salvation from that side. The sharecropper knows that he has no future, either as cropper or day laborer. Once the worker has turned his back on capitalism he instinctively finds his way to socialism and these croppers are no exception.

Such is the development of capitalism that it disciplines, unites, and organizes the workers and shapes their thoughts in the direction of socialism. It is the capitalist state itself which has taught the croppers. The Roosevelt government, fooling the workers and, to some degree, fooling its more naive supporters, has made a great deal of fuss about the La Forge project. This typical piece of liberal window-dressing consists of a settlement for both Negroes and white, although as usual in the South the two are kept apart. Each farmer has 60 acres of land to farm. The government supplies livestock and machinery for common use. Each farm has a good five room house attached to it. Each racial group has a school for the children. There is a co-operative store, where at the end of the year a good percentage on the goods purchased is repaid. Best of all, the government undertakes to buy the crop at a good price. In press and pulpit, on the radio and the political platform, this wonderful piece of work by the Roosevelt government has been trumpeted as one of the outstanding achievements of the New Deal and the beginning of the sharecroppers' paradise on earth.

In reality, it is one of the greatest pieces of humbuggery that you can find. For, of the 20,000 Negroes who work in southeast Missouri, there are about 60 families on the La Forge project. There is a similar number of whites. Maybe when Roosevelt is finished with the war he will think about extending the project, but if the croppers all get farms, where will the landlord get labor? The croppers will get farms when they take them.

One important result, however, has come from the project. It has turned the mind of the most advanced of the sharecroppers in a certain direction. They know what they want. They want sixty acres of land. They want the government to supply the livestock and the tractors and the other machinery to work, to "co-operate" as they phrase it. They want the school and the co-op store. It is a complete social program and it is a socialist program. Though they live and work under conditions which they cannot change by any means that they can see, what distinguishes them from so many workers elsewhere is that they do not aim merely at higher wages and better conditions or honest landlords. They do not want to have anything to do with the old system at all.

The economic and social conditions have driven them far forward in political understanding. They formulate a position on the war with almost Leninist simplicity. "If we get the farms and the schools and the co-op store, then we will fight for our country. Otherwise we have nothing to fight for."

Take the following dialogue. A farmer is asked if he isn't concerned about the fear that Hitler may bomb his house.

"That shack!" he replies with scorn. "That shack should have been bombed 50 years ago."

"But the bomb may kill you."

"What does it matter? I get six bits a day, when I work."

All would not be able to reply so clearly. Among any group of people living in the same conditions there are different levels of development. But that most would respond immediately to these ideas, if clearly and powerfully set before them, is unquestionable.

If they understand the landlord and what he stands for, as far as they are concerned they have no illusions about the Roosevelt government. How could they? Roosevelt has been in power for nearly ten years. What have they to show for it? They know they have only themselves to depend upon. Many of them have at various times joined the UCAPAWA but the locals are not functioning. Periodically Whitfield goes around and makes a speech here and there. But that is about all.

Government relief is given from August to December and consists of beans and graham flour and at other times of graham flour and beans. The graham flour at times is absolutely uneatable even by starving people. At long intervals they will get a pair of overalls or some fat sow belly as meat.

Roosevelt gives them fireside chats, nothing more. What they will get they will have to fight for. For the time being they want $2 a day for an eight hour day when they work as day laborers. They want better relief. They want either money or an order to the store.

Such is their temper and their disillusionment that at the back of their minds most of them are ready for anything. What they need most is organization, the age-old need of the working class. They respect the union, and if the union took any interest in them they would respond. If ever there was an opportunity to start work with the certainty of building a large and powerful organization to struggle for immediate demands and at the same time nourish a consciousness of the new society, it is here.

Despite their many limitations, these workers, in a fundamental sense, are among the most advanced in America. For, to any Marxist, an advanced worker is one who, looking at the system under which he lives, wants to tear it to pieces. That is exactly what the most articulate think of capitalism in southeast Missouri.

III.

The question now is, as always: What is to be done? And that question can only be answered on the basis of what is being done. The answer to what is being done is: Nothing, absolutely nothing.

The Negro sharecroppers are in the UCAPAWA. Probably at different times some 2,500 have joined the union. They rarely pay dues and their poverty is such that this is at least understandable. But every man who has once joined considers himself a member of the union, dues or no dues. They think in terms of the union. To organize them around their union for their immediate demands and militant action is a task that is merely waiting for revolutionary energy, devotion, and understanding.

But the Stalinists are not interested. Periodically they hold a convention. The speeches are made, the program of action outlined. And there it rests. Whitfield, the titular leader, is a parson busy with a church. He is on the union payroll and the Stalinists control the payroll. In case of any dissatisfaction, Whitfield can be depended upon to go around, make a few rousing speeches, and restore his authority and the authority of the union. This was the situation even before the Stalinists started to support Roosevelt's war policy. Today they will be like tigers against anyone who attempts to organize the union for action against the landlords. And here, as elsewhere, it is the greatest delusion to believe that the Stalinists can be exposed by talk, agitation, propaganda, or newspapers. They have to be exposed in action and this is the only way. There is no doubt that this can be done.

During the demonstration, the sharecroppers turned to the Southern Tenant Farmers Union. Butler drove around, telling them to go back—where they were to go back to was not made clear. The croppers understood Butler's role perfectly. "The police tell us to go back. And you, our leader, tell us to go back. What is the difference between you?"

Patient, unobtrusive, careful preparatory work must be done by the more advanced of the men themselves. It will take time. But the difficulties can be conquered. United action on a wide scale is now nothing new to them. With the necessary training, instruction, and patience, there is no reason why a movement should not develop of such power as to sweep away and expose forever in that area the real role of the Stalinists as people who are concerned with nothing else but the plots and maneuvers of the Stalinist bureaucracy in Russia. In that respect the history of the Stalinist party among Chicago Negroes is very instructive.

The ruling class is aware of the dangerous situation. A bill is now before Congress to raise wages and improve working conditions. But such is the social and political power of the landlords that nothing but the organized action of the masses themselves will be able to enforce the most elementary provision, even if it is passed. It is precisely to deal with such paper propositions that the system of terrorism is maintained by the ruling class in the South. It will take more than bills in Congress to help the Southern sharecroppers as it took more than bills and fireside chats to organize the Ford workers. The workers had to get down to business and handle Henry Ford themselves.

Hitherto we have dealt almost exclusively with the Negro sharecroppers and day laborers. But what about the whites? Here is a problem which it is easy to solve in theory but difficult to solve in practice. Years ago the white agricultural worker in the South did not pick or chop cotton. He was above that. But the laws of capitalist decline are merciless and today he is driven to compete with the Negro masses. He is as a rule a little better off. But his general conditions are such that he hates the landlord and the conditions of his existence as fiercely as the Negroes. Yet the two groups of workers are on the whole separate from each other. Some whites are in the union, but the percentage is very small. The union, such as it is, is overwhelmingly Negro.

The white landlords keep up a steady propaganda: "Do not join any union with those blacks. All they want is to get after our white women." But it is idle to believe that this is what keeps white and black agricultural laborers and sharecroppers apart. There is more to it than that. The working whites are an economically privileged group. Jobs as truck drivers, mechanics, etc. are reserved for the whites. When the WPA has jobs to give out, a Negro gets one only after scores of whites have got theirs. The white school teachers get better pay. The white children get better schools. In southeast Missouri the relief authorities will even pass the word around to the whites in a certain area to meet at a certain place, where meat, lard, and clothes are given out while the graham flour and beans are practically all that the Negroes get. It is on this solid, concrete basis that the race prejudice flourishes, not to mention the social advantages which can ease life and nourish pride where life is so hard and degradation so near.

What was the reaction of the whites to the demonstration? Some white families sat down with the demonstrators and a few even went with them to Poplar Bluff. Others came around and told them to stick it out. But a great number said that the Negroes would get nothing by it and were merely being stupid.

What do the Negroes think? Their attitude to these white workers is revolutionary, to the highest degree. The white worker, many of them say, is stupid. He is fooled by the bosses with all this talk about women. If, says one sharecropper to another, these whites were to join with us, we could tear this country to pieces. And a chorus of approval greets his words.

So anxious are they to settle accounts with the landlords that they see in the white workers not their bitter social enemies of many generations, but only possible allies in the class struggle.

Propaganda, education, patient work, will have to be done to knit those elements that draw closer together. But it is the opinion of this writer that so deep-rooted a social phenomenon will only receive a serious shock by the usual way in which all serious problems of the workers' movement are solved or partially solved—by mass action.

Every effort must be made to get all the workers together on a basis of equality. But at present it is the Negro workers who are active, and any rally big action on their part which will have results, will have a tremendous effect on the whites and open the way to a union like the UAW and an organization like the SWOC.

Some time or other that sharecropper-landlord situation is going to explode. Imperialist war, monopoly capitalism, feudalism, and a caste system closer to the Hindu caste system than anything else in the modern world—that is the most dangerous pile of explosives to be found in any regional area of the United States.

The Economics of Lynching (1940)

Marxists have always insisted that lynching has nothing to do with the protection of "the purity of womanhood." The most cursory reading of the evidence collected about lynching shows that the savagery with the Negro is usually charged applies, not to the lynched Negroes, but to the lynchers. Marxists insist further that lynching is rooted in the social and economic conditions of the South. It is not enough to say these things. They must be proved, directly and indirectly.

Some years ago Arthur F. Raper made a careful study of lynching. The results were published in *The Tragedy of Lynching* (University of North Carolina Press, 1933). They are worth study.

The Negroes in the South are most heavily concentrated in the old Black Belt. In this area frequently one half of the population is colored. There the Negro is safer from lynching than anywhere else. Why? Says Raper, "In the Black Belt race relations revolve about the plantation system, under which the Negro tenants and wage hands are practically indispensable. Here the variant economic and cultural levels of the mass of whites and the mass of Negroes are well defined and far removed." The December 1939 number of *The New International* contains a long and well-documented article by Robert Birchman that analyzes these conditions, and shows the Negro's status to be little removed from the slavery of pre-Civil War days. Tied hand and foot by the economic system, kept in his place by the laws of capitalist production, the Negro is lynched least in these areas.

The lynchings that do occur, however, are of a special type, corresponding to the economic set-up and the political and social conditions created by it.

"The Black Belt lynching is something of a business transaction," writes Arthur Raper. "The whites there, chiefly of the planter class and consciously dependent upon the Negro for labor, lynch him to conserve traditional landlord-tenant relations rather than to wreak vengeance upon his race.

Black Belt white men demand that the Negroes stay out of their politics and dining room, the better to keep them in their fields and kitchens."

There is not "widespread hysteria." The mob is usually small. In cases examined by Raper, the "mob proceeded in routine fashion . . . with almost clock-like precision." In these areas politics is the white employer's business. The Negro must not interfere. The county officials are direct agents of the plantation owners and are well paid. The sheriff of Bolivar County, for instance, received in 1931 $40,000 a year, ten times the salary of the governor of Mississippi. "In these Black Belt plantation areas, where modified slave patterns still persist, any crime which occurs among the propertyless Negroes is considered a labor matter to be handled by the white landlord or his overseer."

We see now why these fellows are so fiercely opposed to the anti-lynching bill. It will be a powerful means of awakening the Negroes to the fact that they have rights which are recognized, in theory at any rate, by the Federal Government. The bill will not stop lynching but it will strike a blow at the whole system.

Frank Shay, in his book *Judge Lynch* (Ives Washburn, 1938), gives a picture of the other type of lynching, where the mob grows wild and tears the living flesh from the burning Negro. This mob, he says, is made up of young men between their teens and their middle twenties with a sprinkling of morons of all ages. "Its members are native whites, mostly of the underprivileged, the unemployed, the dispossessed, and the unattached. . . . They are grocery-clerks, soda-jerks, low-paid employees in jobs that require neither training nor intelligence; jobs that might often be filled more competently by Negroes and at lower wages. In rural communities this mob is made up of day workers and wage-hands, the more shiftless type of tenants, those who through birth and former position are bound to the locality."

There we have it. Their own misery, defeat, and the fear for the scraps by which they live drive them periodically to terrorize and wreak their wrath against the social system on the Negroes, whom they see as their greatest enemy, and whom they are traditionally taught to despise. Here again lynching is rooted in the economic system and even the very forms it takes are conditioned by the specific class relations of the two races.

Raper illustrates this principle in many ways. Take the situation in North Texas and Central Oklahoma. This is not a Black Belt area, and in the urban communities of these counties many business and professional Negroes own comfortable homes and other property. A considerable proportion of the colored people regularly participate in local and national elections. The propertied whites, not dependent upon Negro labor as are the whites in the Black belt area, do not circumscribe the Negro's activity to the same degree. But the poorer whites in the rural areas are hostile. By violence and threats they drive the Negroes from the rural neighborhoods. The lynch-mobs number over one thousand.

Raper makes one truly astonishing observation. While the propertied whites here allow the Negroes a certain freedom, they do not need them for labor and are therefore indifferent to Negro persecution by the poor whites. In the Black Belt, however, the plantation owners protect their Negro serfs from the hostility of the poor whites. They are not going to have their labor force interfered with by a rival labor force. When there is any lynching to be done, they themselves will do it, in a systematic and organized manner.

One last point. Going on data compiled by Woofter, Raper shows that between 1900 and 1930, whenever the price of cotton is above the usual trend, the number of lynchings is below the average. Whenever the price of cotton is depressed, the number of lynchings increases.

The Fourth International struggles wherever a battle in the class war is being waged. We utilize the capitalist parliament for our own purposes, and that is why we do all we can do to defeat the attempt of the Senators to block the anti-lynching bill. But we never lose sight of the fact that the greatest enemy of all is the capitalist system. It cannot exist in the South without mob law. The workers, black and white, must steadily prepare to destroy capitalism, the root source of lynching.

THE RACE POGROMS AND THE NEGRO (1943)

Gloom and despair have gripped millions of the Negro population of this country. For at least a year the coming explosions were a topic of conversation everywhere. They were written about extensively in the Negro press and in certain sections of the capitalist press as well. Masses of the Negro people had shown their determination, their courage, their willingness to sacrifice, on every possible occasion that an opportunity presented itself. Yet the blow has fallen upon them and they have been powerless to meet it. Not only that. They expect, and with good reason, that more desperate times are ahead. This is not a matter of a long-range program for abolishing the economic and social basis of race prejudice. The problem is much more urgent than that. Events in states as far apart as Florida, California, Pennsylvania, Texas, Michigan, and New York have shown that at any moment gangs of whites will begin to beat up and murder Negroes in the streets, and to wreck and burn down blocks of Negro homes. Yet the helplessness with which the Negroes watched the peril approach shows quite clearly that though they, above all people, realize how urgent the problem is, they are still not aware of the real forces at work against them, and therefore cannot plan to meet the emergency. Now, while they are searching everywhere for a way out of the danger, we propose to place before them and their friends certain fundamental facts of the present situation and to draw certain conclusions from those facts.

The first and most important point is that it is useless to depend on the government for protection. By the government we mean the Washington administration under Roosevelt or whoever may be President, the Department of Justice, the FBI, the senators and congressmen, the state administrations, the state governors, the city police, the Fair Employment Practices Commission (FEPC), all forms and manner of official power. These will not—and, being what they are, cannot—protect the Negro people.

First, the Administration in Washington. The Roosevelt government knew that the Detroit outbreak was on the way. After the rioting in 1942 over the Sojourner Truth housing project, government investigators reported on the general situation as follows: "It is not melodrama when city officials here [in Detroit] say this conflict is the most serious the city has faced since well before the time of the big strikes. They don't go far enough in what they say. It would be nearer realism to say that, if not today, tomorrow, this country, or let us say the war effort, will face its biggest crisis all over the North!"

The investigator referred specifically to Buffalo and Philadelphia as danger points.

"A person not in the vortex of the situation can hardly realize its urgency. Therefore, let it be repeated once more: it is beyond control and extends far beyond Detroit, and unless strong and quick intervention by some high official, preferably the President, is taken at once, hell is going to be let loose in every Northern city where large numbers of Negroes are in competition."

We will not go into the question here of whether immigrants or the Ku Klux Klanners are mainly responsible for the outbreaks in Detroit. It is sufficient to note that, whoever they are, in the Northern cities at least, they are a definite minority even among the workers. Remember also that the government today wants no interruption in war production. Yet rather than take steps to protect the Negroes, it preferred to let the situation rest as it was. In connection with the Sojourner Truth riot, the government arrested three men on a charge of "seditious conspiracy." This was in February 1942. Today, eighteen months later, the government has not brought them to trial. To depend on this government for protection is suicide.

Now mark what happened during the riots. The police are the local representatives of the state. To them is entrusted the power of the state in its dealings with civilians. Their duty is supposedly to protect the lives and property of civilians who are lawlessly attacked. But the police cannot be expected to act in one way when the government, from whom they derive their authority, acts in another. Their actions, therefore, merely show crudely what is the real policy of the government. *They sided with the rioters!* Every Negro and every friend of elementary human decency should frame and display in his house that shameful photograph in which two policemen hold a Negro while a white rioter hits him in the face, and a third policeman on a horse looks on. That the police, the power of the state, is in this conspiracy against the Negro people has penetrated into the head even of Walter White, national secretary of the NAACP. He writes from Detroit on June 23: "Twenty five of the 28 who lie dead from the race rioting are Negroes. One hundred percent of the 32 who were tried and convicted of rioting yesterday were Negroes. In these figures lies the answer to the sullenness and bitter despair I saw yesterday on the faces of Negroes."

Of the twenty-four Negroes killed, twenty were killed directly by the shots of the police. The lives of the Negroes were in far more danger from the government's representatives than from the rioters. The triggers were pressed by the fingers of Detroit policemen, but the guns were aimed by the government in Washington. For the Roosevelt government has shown the policemen quite clearly where it stood in regard to Negroes. It had not only segregated them in the Army, the Navy, the Air Force, and the federal government itself, thereby making it impossible for policemen to have the proper respect for the rights of Negroes; by the government's action over the Sojourner Truth riots, by its refusal to take one single step to avert the crisis which everybody, and particularly the police, knew was on the way, the government had given the police a clear direction as to where the guns were to be pointed.

The government in all its shapes and forms is responsible for these murderous attacks, not only before they occurred, but while they were going on. On Monday, June 22, two hundred and fifty representatives of labor, fraternal, and social organizations, *both Negro and white*, crowded into the dining room of the Lucy Thurman YWCA at noon in order to take measures to protect the Negro people. Speaker after speaker indicted the police for murdering Negroes, for concentrating on Negro areas, for refusing to arrest the leaders of the white mobs. They gave examples from their own personal observation. They called on Mayor Jeffries, who was present, to put an end to this lawlessness by the state. They asked him to go on the radio and warn that all instigators would be severely punished. They condemned his handling of the situation.

Jeffries refused point-blank to take the actions they recommended. The latest news is that both Jeffries and the FBI have agreed that there is no need for any investigation. In Los Angeles, the city police joined with the rioters against the Mexicans and Negroes. After the Mobile outbreak, Monsignor Haas, new head of the FEPC, another government body, recommended that the Negroes be segregated into four Jim Crow shipyards which make only bare hulls. This means that, though Negroes can become shipfitters, welders, and drillers, they will be barred from such highly skilled and highly paid work as machine operating, pipe fitting, and electrical installation. By this action, rioters are told by the government that if they riot hard enough they can be sure of attaining their substantial demands: to "keep the Negro in his place." From Texas, a writer for the newspaper *PM* reports what is common knowledge: that the state guard and police in Beaumont, as all over the South, resented the fact that they were called upon to defend Negroes against white men. And it is no longer a question of only the South.

The Situation in New York

New York has long been known as one of the places where segregation is practiced least (that is the best that can be said), and Mayor LaGuardia is reputed to be one of the great friends of the Negro. Some weeks ago the Mayor gave his assent to a Metropolitan Insurance Housing Project which will exclude Negroes. Thus, at this critical time, the head of the city administration gives to would-be rioters and to his own city police an unequivocal demonstration of his attitude on the race question. The city police understood their Mayor even before he spoke. On June 24, at a meeting of the City Council, Councilman Clayton Powell, a Negro, said that New York had recently witnessed "a continuous succession of unwarranted brutality perpetrated upon Negro citizens in our city," with many cases resulting in deaths. He had taken each of these cases up by mail with Police Commissioner Valentine. One letter had been acknowledged, the rest had been ignored. "I now say, fellow councilmen," continued Powell, "that the riots of Detroit can easily be duplicated here in New York City. The blood of innocent people, white and Negro, will rest upon the hands of Mayor Fiorello LaGuardia and Police Commissioner Valentine, who have refused to see representative citizens to discuss means of combatting outbreaks in New York." What protection can be expected from such a police force?

The Negro people, therefore, had better make up their minds. The state, the government, in Washington, Detroit, New York, Los Angeles, or anywhere else, is no protection. There will be some talk. The government may send in some troops after the mischief has been done and the situation seems to be spreading too far. It may even appoint a commission. But before, during, and after the rioting, the government and its agents act in accordance with the three hundred-year-old policy of American capitalism—nor could it be otherwise. The state, says Marx, is the executive committee of the ruling class. The American capitalist class has gained untold riches by its specially brutal exploitation of Negroes. To deaden the consciousness of exploitation among the white workers it taught them to despise Negroes. Today it needs uninterrupted production for its war. But when certain backward elements among the whites attack Negroes, the capitalist class, through its executive committee, the state, shows that even against its own immediate war interests, it must continue that persecution upon which so much of its power and privileges have been built. The Army, the Navy, the police, the Department of Justice—all these are the instruments whereby the capitalist class holds down the masses of the people. They are soaked in race prejudice as a matter of policy. Even if the government dislikes race riots, it cannot take vigorous steps to repress them because that will tear down the prejudice on which so much depends. If Negroes depend on the government, they are going to be dragged from trolleys and beaten up; they and their wives and children will be shot down by rioters and police; and their homes will be wrecked and burned. Furthermore, these riots are no passing phase. Even if, by some miracle, they are held in check during the war, when the war is over they will burst forth with tenfold intensity.

The Bishop and the Uncle Toms

Two weeks before the Detroit outburst, the Right Reverend C. Ransom, bishop of the African Methodist Episcopal Church, addressed a meeting of 1500 people in Town Hall, New York. The bishop spoke to a people strongly conscious of the danger which hung over them. He made one reference to the work of the President and "his great wife" for Negro equality, but he called upon the Negro people to fight. He made a public confession. "I am tired of lying and compromising. We praise William Lloyd Garrison— he was a white man who died for the Negro—but Negroes must learn to die for themselves!" He concluded: "I'd rather die and be damned than to surrender my absolute equality to any man!" The bishop is a little shaky on the theology. We can assure him on the very highest authority that if he were to die fighting for equality he will at least not be damned. But his political line is impeccable.

What makes his speech so noteworthy is that, in all the outpourings of the wordy Negro leaders in this crisis, his stands almost alone. With all that had happened and the prospects of still worse to come, not one of the so-called leaders of the Negro people had the courage, the sense, or the honesty to call upon the people to defend themselves. We shall give a selection of what they did say, so that there will be some record of the shameful cowardice, self-seeking, and bankruptcy of these betrayers of the Negro masses. (The selections are all from the June 26 issues.)

The People's Voice

"It is evident that the Axis is planning an invasion of America. . . . Our government has been mysteriously soft-hearted in dealing with the big-time fifth columnists of America. . . . It is time the President of the United States stopped phony investigations of lynching, police brutality, maltreatment of black soldiers, mob law, and got down to business. . . ." Then, in large capitals: "THE QUESTION THAT NOW CONCERNS US IS NOT— WILL WE WIN THE PEACE, BUT WILL WE WIN THE WAR? AND IF SO, WHICH ONE? ABROAD OR AT HOME? Signed, Adam Clayton Powell."

To the people in Buffalo, Philadelphia, and elsewhere, wondering when their turn will come, it must be comforting to know that the Axis is planning an invasion of America and that is why their heads are being busted open.

• *The New York Age*: "The saturation point is fast being reached. The failure of legal authorities to face the situation is bringing nearer and nearer that fatal day when the limit of human endurance shall have been reached. . . . If and when that day is allowed to come, there will be trouble."

• *The Pittsburgh Courier*: "We urge prompt and immediate action by the Office of the Attorney General. . . . The Federal Bureau of Investigation. . . . Nazi saboteurs, Axis inspired!" Then, in large print: "WE DEMAND ACTION."

• *The Chicago Defender*: "Let us still further unify our country and go forward to win the war NOW in 1943."

• *The Journal and Guide*: "The state governments must play their part; the city and county governments must play their part; if they fail the federal government must assume its responsibility as was done in the Detroit case. It is time for America to close ranks if we are to retain the respect of the other members of the United Nations. . . ."

You see, it is not Negro lives which are at stake, but the respect for America of the United Nations.

Lester Granger (for the National Urban League) in a telegram to President Roosevelt: "We therefore call on you to order an immediate investigation of these outbreaks and the possibility of their subversive instigation. . . ."

Walter White (for the NAACP) in a telegram to President Roosevelt: "We urge you to go on the radio at the earliest possible moment and appeal to America to resist Axis and other propaganda. . . ."

Ferdinand Smith (chairman) and Charlie Collins (secretary), Negro Labor Victory Committee: "We feel that the Detroit outbreak demands most stringent measures to prevent the further breakdown of morale and war production."

These are the Negro leaders. These are the cringing, crawling, whining Uncle Toms who have not addressed a single manifesto to the Negro people and to their white fellow citizens, many of whom are, in organizations or singly, ready to do what they can for the defense of the Negro people.

No. It is to that very President, to those very legal authorities, who have themselves so criminally, by commission and omission, encouraged and protected the rioters—it is to them that these Negro leaders address themselves, beating the big drum against the Axis. Read those extracts again. What they are saying is this: "Don't you see, Mr. President, that when they shoot us down and bust our heads open, it stops our war production? If it wasn't for that, we wouldn't trouble you."

The President is the same man who so shocked Walter White by openly supporting segregation in the armed forces, who has used the FEPC as a toy windmill to fool Negroes; the same who, according to Adam Clayton Powell, has instigated phony investigations into the thousands of government-organized brutalities perpetrated against the Negro people every day. So far, the President has kept quiet. As long as he can have Walter White, Lester Granger, and Ferdinand Smith to keep the Negroes quiet, why should be say anything? However, Eleanor Roosevelt has not the gift of silence. When the zoot-suit riots broke out, she was in Washington, the center of government. The world will little note or long remember what she did there. She did nothing. But she said plenty. As a fitting crown to a notably platitudinous career she declared that "Americans must sooner or later face the fact that we have a race problem." The words are not an indictment of Eleanor Roosevelt. This pouring of little thimblefuls of water on great fires is her job. But the colossal insolence and contempt of her remarks is an indictment of the Walter Whites, the Lester Grangers, and the Ferdinand Smiths. It will be an everlasting tribute to their role as *de facto* agents of the white ruling class among the Negro people that, in this crisis, not one of them turned to the Negroes and said: "Negroes, defend yourselves."

Two voices, and two voices only, spoke up clearly on the riots in general, if not actually on Detroit. The first was the *Afro-American* of Baltimore, which, commenting on the Texas riots, spoke words which should be learned by heart. Every sentence is pregnant with wisdom:

> The cause of the attack upon the hundreds of innocent colored people is not important. Some Southern communities need no incentive to mob action. All they want is an excuse. In a situation like this in the South, it is idle to appeal either to state or federal authorities for assistance. It usually comes too late. Colored communities must be prepared to protect themselves. Frederick Douglass said that the slave who resisted vigorously was almost never whipped. If mobsters attacking colored homes get a hot reception once, they will not repeat that visit.

The second, the *Amsterdam News* of New York, was still more powerful:

> We knew and we have said repeatedly that there can be no law and order (Negroes really don't care whether whites like them or not) in the United States until the federal government steps in and stops the continuous program of pogroms perpetrated against Negro citizens, particularly in

the South. By failing to protect the lives and security of American citizens, our government tacitly enters into what amounts to collusion with the Nazi-minded and acting whites of America. Conditions between the two races are now so bad that any sane citizen fears not only for his country, but for his family, friends, and himself.

Because our government refuses to act resolutely—to go in and punish the mob members, regardless of their number—it is now mandatory on every citizen to protect himself. To protect oneself in face of mob violence means to fight back hard without giving any quarter to anyone. This may mean death but it's far, far better to die fighting as a man than to perish like a caged animal in Beaumont or elsewhere.

Unfortunately, the Negro citizen's war is right here at home, against white mobs. Let us battle them unto death, until our government, dedicated to protecting all of its citizens, does its duty as any government worth its salt would. The die is cast and we must fight all the way for our lives, our homes, and our self-respect.

That is the whole thing in a nutshell. There are some thirteen million Negroes in this country. They are willing and anxious to defend themselves. In their place, who would not be? We ask the Negroes: shouldn't Ferdinand Smith, Lester Granger, Walter White, and all the Negro press have joined in a common manifesto to the Negro people? Shouldn't they have called upon them to defend themselves, and denounced by name the President, the police officers, the legal authorities, the mayors, and all others who have so criminally encouraged and aided, directly and indirectly, in the persecution of the Negro people? Shouldn't they have appealed to the great body of white people in this country, telling them that in view of the shameless failure to protect Negroes, it was up to the citizens themselves to do it? Any Negro leader who cannot answer in the affirmative to the above questions is a traitor to his people and should be driven out from among them.

Every school club, every street, every church group, can organize for defense where official authority has failed them, as it now has. They can pool their resources and train defense guards. The movement should be nation-wide and it could be started tomorrow.

Should the President be ignored? Not at all. The President should be informed, not by weekly telegrams about the Axis, but by tens of thousands of citizens marching on Washington. Walter White and Philip Randolph bear a direct responsibility for the helpless situation the masses of the Negroes find themselves in today. When the people were ready to march on

Washington, they cringed before Roosevelt and LaGuardia and called off the march. Is it any wonder that the state has continued its contemptuous course? Only one thing will make it change, and that is when it sees that the Negro masses are not listening to those who continually present their behinds to be kicked, but are themselves undertaking their own defense, and are presenting their ills to the government in person.

Some of these cowards and hangers-on to the Roosevelt government whisper that "we Negroes cannot fight the whole white population." The statement is a gross slander against tens of millions of white people in America—and above all a slander of the Congress of Industrial Organizations (CIO). We ask the Negro people to note that, during the last ten weeks, the whole bungling, hypocritical administration set-up for placing the burdens of the war upon the masses has been exposed and made to totter by the magnificent action of the miners on strike. These half-million men have trusted in their union, and not in the state, which they have recognized for what it is—the executive committee of the ruling class. They have shown what well-organized, determined men can do. One hundred thousand of them are Negroes. Yet nobody thinks of white miners and Negro miners. They are just "the miners." The reason is because the Negro miners are perfectly integrated into the labor movement. This is what the Negroes must aim at. They must integrate themselves as tightly as possible into the labor movement. It is true that even in the CIO some white workers are hostile to Negroes, such as those who struck at the Packard plant against the up-grading of Negroes. But the United Auto Workers (UAW) of Detroit, for instance, has repeatedly demonstrated its sympathy with the Negroes against the comparatively small section of Detroit race-baiters. It has repeatedly condemned the mayor of Detroit for his criminal laxity. Let the Negroes note this, and where, as in Detroit, they are strongly represented in the unions, let them make direct appeal to the unions for help in the organization of the defense. There are difficulties in the way. But the Negroes can overcome them if they first depend upon themselves and then call for the direct support of labor.

Walter Reuther, vice-president of the UAW, has said: "As soon as they pull the troops out of here it will happen again. Our only hope is that some active committee is organized to arouse the decent people of this town so that this won't happen again." R. J. Thomas, president of the UAW, has stupidly complained that the auto manufacturers "have given us little cooperation in helping to smooth race relations." That remark is in its way as miserable as the telegrams of Walter White and Lester Granger to Roosevelt. But the union leaders are undoubtedly bitter about the whole savage business and know the danger which it represents for union solidarity. Let the Negro community and particularly the Negro workers in the unions put the problems squarely to the unions themselves. "We cannot trust the state, in Washington or here. You are the most powerful organized force in the community. We are, most of us, workers like yourselves. We are organizing for our own defense and we appeal to you." If only the workers see that the Negroes mean business, they are certain to respond. But the Negroes must first rid themselves of the misleaders who are always looking to Roosevelt, or to Pearl Buck, or to Wendell Willkie, for help—and also, incidentally, for the publicity which it brings. *If the Negroes do not defend themselves, it is certain nobody else will.* . . .

White Workers' Prejudices (1945)

This column will attempt to describe some of the social reasons for the antagonism of the white worker to the Negro. While the antagonism is basically due to the system of capitalism, there are obvious ways in which Jim Crow makes itself felt.

First, whites and Negroes are segregated in the communities in which they live. The mass of Negroes the white workers has occasion to observe occupy an inferior and degraded position.

The Negroes whom he happens to meet are as a rule poor, shabby, often belonging to the dregs of the population. There are many whites who belong to the dregs of the population also. But counteracting these are the whites who are rich, powerful, well educated; besides the number who are just ordinary citizens, neither rich nor dregs, but fulfilling in their various ways the social functions of society.

If in a particular community there are Negroes who have achieved a certain education and competence, they function almost exclusively in relation to the Negro community. The ordinary white worker is only vaguely aware of their existence.

A worker never goes into an insurance office, or a department store, or a lawyer's office where he sees a Negro or Negroes occupying positions of authority, or giving evidence of knowledge, or receiving the consideration which is due to those who have achieved the status of the middle class. For the daily round of his life Negroes for the most part, if not menials, are entertainers, singers, dancers, or players of jazz music.

These concrete realities are reinforced by the literature and art of the system. The worker does not create these. He does not ask for anti-Negro literature. As workers do in every country, he reads the books, newspapers, and goes to the shows. From every one of these organs of communication and education his daily impressions about Negroes are reinforced. Movies reflect the society in which they are produced. The white worker constantly sees the Negro on the screen in situations which merely confirm his knowledge of the realities he himself has experienced.

In books and magazines, all grace, strength, beauty, nobility, courage are automatically attributed to members of the white race. It isn't that the books are openly or even subtly anti-Negro. It is that in the mental and emotional stimulation which they provide, good or bad, the Negro is usually excluded. If he is included, he is placed in his usual menial position, made the butt of jokes or at the very best is portrayed as a good and loyal servant.

The process does not end there. The whole history of the nation, the background of its thought, its social customs as expressed in the *unconscious* attitudes and sense of values of even people who are not personally hostile to Negroes—all these are permeated by the national attitude to the Negro people. Take an apparently simple thing like a brilliant performance in any sphere by a Negro. A well-meaning reporter will say with a certain satisfaction that the individual in question is a Negro.

He means well, but the mere statement of the fact carries with it the connotation that it is an exceptional thing for a Negro to show exceptional merit. A white man or woman who is friendly with a Negro is conscious that he or she risks criticism, or at any rate comment, from most of his friends.

This is the daily, inescapable experience of the average American white worker.

The productive system of the United States created the basis of the Negro situation and it is the productive system which is creating the basis of its solution. It is the mass production industries which have within recent years placed whites and Negroes together on a basis of equality in that most fundamental social sphere—the process of productive labor.

Even though segregation (into the lowest jobs) pursued the Negro there, yet the discipline of large-scale production welded blacks and whites into a unit. It was on this that the fraternal unity of blacks and whites in the

CIO was founded. It could have been founded and can be maintained on no other basis.

The social forces and customs making for division between whites and Negroes are too powerful to be seriously affected except by some such powerful discipline and unity as are imposed by the productive process itself. In the past the competition between workers was a fruitful source of maintaining the division. It will be more dangerous in the future. But if the unions tackle the struggle for full employment as a struggle for which both employed and unemployed workers must be mobilized, then what has been a cause of division in the past can be a source of even greater unity in the future.

The Rapid Growth of the NAACP (1947)

The NAACP, I am informed, now has close to one million members. I doubt if many people know this. And I am pretty certain that if they do, few except the Marxists can understand what it means. It is one of the surest signs of the insoluble social crisis in the United States.

This growth has taken place during the last 12 years. In 1935, the membership was quite insignificant. In 1939, it was about 300,000. By 1943, it was half a million. And now, in 1947, it is almost one million. The Negro population is only 15 million. There is a small number of whites in the NAACP. The large majority of the membership is Negro. And when one out of every fifteen of the Negroes in the United States joins an organization aiming at the destruction of Negro oppression and discrimination, that becomes an indication of a tremendous social ferment in the nation as a whole.

What is it that has moved these Negroes to this tremendous mobilization? The answer is simple. There is obviously a dislocation of the whole social order which drives them towards unifying their forces for struggle. They are impelled toward the search for solidarity because they realize that all the great problems of the nation and of the Negro minority are now being posed. They gird themselves for a solution of their own.

Look at those two dates again, 1935 to 1947. To any Marxist student of American life, those dates must immediately call to mind the formation of the Congress of Industrial Organizations (CIO). Precisely during this time when the Negroes were just beginning to organize themselves, the labor movement of the United States accomplished one of the most astonishing mobilizations in the history of the working class.

The proletariat, in some of its deepest layers, felt that the foundations of American society were cracking under its feet, instinctively the long-overdue organization of industrial unions appeared out of the depths of dislocated capitalist society. If the CIO is a response of labor to the crisis of American society, then the organization of the Negroes in the NAACP is a response which has the same roots. Both were the reaction of Americans to the crisis of the American environment.

The NAACP response is not so much a Negro as an American phe-nomenon. But precisely because these Americans are Negroes, the mass mobilizations assume the astounding ratio of roughly one out of every fifteen Negroes in the nation. The Negroes are more bitterly oppressed, more disgusted, more humiliated, than any other section of the population. That is the reason why they react so strongly to the stimuli of disintegrating society.

That is what is important, the mass movement towards organizations. It expresses the sense that the conditions are intolerable; that the possibility of change exists; that it is necessary to act. Whenever hundreds of thousands of people take action of any significant kind, that is an infallible sign of social contradictions expressing themselves.

That being said, however, it is now possible to say certain other things. The NAACP, as led by Walter White and his fellow-fakers, is an orga-nization miserably inadequate for the great cause it is designed to serve. For years, it has distinguished itself by its inability to mobilize its followers for mass action. It has done useful work in publicizing such barbarisms as lynching. It has fought cases in the courts. It has carried out a strictly legalistic type of propaganda and agitation.

Militant Negroes have long recognized the NAACP's fear of mass action. Today the same leaders are in the saddle and with their long training, they undoubtedly wish nothing more than to carry on in the manner which has distinguished them in the past.

But history is overtaking them. An organization of one million is vastly different from an organization of one thousand. Furthermore, the Negro population in the United States is predominately proletarian or semi-proletarian. The moment you read a ratio like 1 in 15, it means that a substantial number of that million consists of working class families.

The very size of the organization gives confidence to its membership. They have not joined in order to send more telegrams to Washington or to make more cases before the Supreme Court. They want action. The NAACP is therefore in a state of turmoil. The membership is pressing for action. The leadership searches for some sort of program. It is impossible to give any forecast as to what the result will be.

For the time being, however, this much can be said. The fate of the extraordinary mass movement rests with the great social forces of the nation. This growth of the NAACP is not an accident; it represents the Negro mobilization following World War II which corresponds to the Negro mobilization that followed World War I. That mobilization was the Garvey movement. It took the extravagant form that it did precisely because there was not at that time in the United States an organized labor movement which could stand before the nation as the potential leader of all the oppressed. Today, that is not so.

The Negro people as a whole believe in the CIO more than they believe in any social organization in the nation. In the industrial towns many of the members of the NAACP are good union men. Their education in the union movement has not lessened, but sharpened, their consciousness of their oppression as Negroes. They have heretofore joined the struggle of the NAACP as the most convenient medium for carrying on their own special struggle. It was the social crisis which precipitated the CIO into existence. It was the social crisis which has precipitated the phenomenal growth of the NAACP.

The deepening of the crisis will drive the American proletariat on to the road of political action on a scale corresponding to the social explosion which was the CIO. Any such movement will most certainly bring in its train convulsions in the NAACP. The solidity of American capitalist society is undermined, and under our eyes the forces that are to overthrow it are slowly but surely preparing themselves for the gigantic explosions which will usher in the actual revolutionary crisis.

THREE

The Politics of Culture

I.

Eighty million Americans visit the cinema every week, and in the course of the next year or so, perhaps ninety million will see the film *Gone With the Wind*. Millions will get from this film their most powerful impression of the greatest civil war in history and one of the decisive turning points in modern history.

What will they see? At the very start we are informed that the film is a tribute to the "grace and gallantry" of a vanished civilization—"the age of chivalry." The South was a "land of grace and plenty" (our quotations are literal). The Civil War took place, God knows why: as far as can be made out from the film, owing to the hotheadedness and chivalrous gallantry of the Southern cavaliers; and the Southerners lost because, blinded by their excessively martial qualities, they did not notice that they had no munitions factories.

Of the slaves themselves, old O'Hara tells Scarlett, "You must be firm, but you must be gentle, especially with darkies." And Negroes, not only the house-servants but the field hands, are all faithful unto death. Negroes are all right—so long as they are kept in their places. Of the old Negro mammy, Rhett Butler says that there are few persons whose respect he so much values. When Scarlett O'Hara sees the faithful Negro man-servant in tears, she says, "I can stand anybody's tears but yours." When Ashley remonstrates with Scarlett, about exploiting white convicts, she retorts that he wasn't so particular about owning slaves. Ashley replies that slavery was different: we treated them well, and besides, he intended to free all his. When Scarlett is attacked by louts, a white and a Negro, it is a Negro, a former slave, who rescues her at great danger to himself.

Of the carpetbaggers, robbers of the South in Southern mythology, we get a brief but emphatic indication with a particularly gaudy and fat-looking carpetbag to symbolize Northern rapacity. And, glory be to the God of History, the Negro ex-slave who rescues Scarlett is thankful to leave the South because he has had enough of these carpetbaggers.

Incredible as it may sound, the decisive result of the war, the abolition of slavery, is not directly mentioned in over three hours. The South would not have been able to stand that. And for good reason. As an article by Robert Birchman on Southern agriculture (in the December 1939 issue of *New International*) shows, the essentials of Negro slavery still remain over large parts of the South.

The picture is a stimulus to the old prejudices and hatred which were the natural outcome of chattel slavery and which must continue on the basis of the sharecropping system of today. Writing in the *Amsterdam News* of 23 December 1939, St. Clair Bourne notes "the fond illusions of the days of slavery" reinforced in many Southern whites since they have seen the picture at the Atlanta premiere. Bourne reports that a Negro girl who takes care of two little white boys, one of them eight and the other ten, noticed that on the morning after the premiere they acted strangely to her. On being questioned, the elder said he had overheard his parents, who had seen the film, discussing slavery and the Civil War. This small boy continued, "You'd be a slave too, if it wasn't for the Yankees. And then my Daddy wouldn't have to pay you . . ."

Even in the making of this picture, the natural resentment of the Negroes showed itself. The *Pittsburgh Courier* claims that the script as originally written was even more offensive to the Negro people and it was only because of the *Courier* agitation that some of the offending parts were taken out. The *Amsterdam News*, 18 December 1939, states that during production many Negroes, irritated at the role that was attributed to their people, refused to go on with their parts; there were quarrels and even fist fights.

The historical statements and implications of the picture are false from the beginning to the end. A few thousand slaveholders in the South exploited the millions of slaves, while a few thousand others bred slaves for the slave market as today people breed horses and dogs. If house servants were often treated kindly, the majority, the Negroes in the field, were worked to death and terrorized in order to be kept in submission. By the middle of the nineteenth century the slave system was bankrupt. But the slaveowners wanted to establish their domination over the country in order to shape its course for no other purpose than the maintenance of their rotting and reactionary system. The Northern industrialists, in that age progressive, crushed the South because the South was a check on capitalist production. In the war 220,000 Negroes fought on the Northern side.

That was the Civil War. It is the duty of all revolutionaries wherever possible to point out the gross historical falsifications of this picture, and to do all in their power to counteract the pernicious influence that it is likely to have on the minds of the people, who, knowing no better, may be tempted to accept this as history.

II.

The Stalinists are now whipping up a furious campaign on *Gone With the Wind*. Their methods are an exact replica of the methods of the Moscow bureaucracy. When Stalin decides to shoot some thousands of Old Bolsheviks, or to denounce Germany (or to praise Germany), or to invade Finland, there suddenly appear in the Moscow press letters, resolutions, exhortations, praising the particular move, extolling it as the highest wisdom, and pointing out that this is exactly what the Soviet workers have been waiting for. Similarly with the Communist Party in every country.

On its issue of 5 January 1940 the *Daily Worker* prints nearly two columns of letters, of which the following quotation characterizes the tone: "Well, I simply can't hold it back any longer. Your excellent and Marxist handling of that smelly film *Gone With the Wind* was sparkling . . . ." The whole Stalinist community, we are made to understand, is simply boiling with rage at the slanders against the Negro people embodied in the film.

Gone With the Wind, however, is not the first film that deals with Negro conditions in the Old South. A little knowledge will be sufficient to show that, behind all this noisy parade, the Stalinists, here as elsewhere, are deceiving the Negro people, and serving exclusively the interests of their paymasters in the Kremlin.

Some ten years ago, when the Moscow bureaucracy had not yet entirely broken with the revolutionary doctrines of Lenin and Trotsky, it invited some Negroes to Moscow to make a film which would depict lynching and the other features of Negro life in America. The company was selected and reached Moscow. American capitalism, however, realizes that, although it can deceive the people at home, it would be difficult for it to pose abroad as the friend of democracy if its treatment of Negroes were exposed in so popular a medium as a film. Washington was at that time engaged in negotiations with Moscow over recognition of the Soviet government, and made it quite clear that if the Russians made any such film, it would be regarded as a serious obstacle in the way of an understanding.

The Moscow bureaucracy reacted in characteristic fashion. It capitulated before the capitalists. It sought to deceive and browbeat the workers. The Negroes who had gone to Moscow were told that it was impossible for the Soviet production studios to find time and room to make the film. When some of the Negroes protested, several attempts were made to frame them as drunkards, disorderly persons, etc. in order to discredit in advance any protest that they might make when they returned home. In all this the *Daily Worker*, which now cannot contain its rage at Hollywood's crimes, played its usual obedient and servile role as a tout for the Kremlin's crimes.

Among the Negroes who went to Moscow to help in the making of the film was Langston Hughes, the Negro poet. Hughes is one of the most pertinacious fellow-travellers of the Stalinists. He is, or was, vice-president of their stooge organization, the American Writers Congress. He has represented the Stalinist point of view at international congresses in Europe. Some of his works are published by Stalinist publishing houses. When the Moscow bureaucracy tried to impose its lies on the Negroes who had gone to Moscow to make the Negro film, he accepted the "explanation" entirely and cooperated with the Moscow bureaucrats, to smash down those who refused to accept this transparent lie.

But the Kremlin's policy changes, and with it changes everything, from the clothes the Stalinists wear to their attitude to Negro films. Not so long ago Hollywood wanted to produce a film on the Old South. *Way Down South* portrayed the old Southern slaveowners as fine and gallant gentlemen, and showed the slaves as being contented with their slavery. One of the writers of the script was no other than Langston Hughes. Of this the Stalinists, who must have known it, had nothing whatever to say.

Now the line of the Kremlin changes once more. Their reviewer, Howard Rushmore, wrote a favorable review which, in this opinion of the author of this column, was infinitely less iniquitous than the actual preparation of a pro-slavery script. But the Stalinists become consumed with virtuous rage, dismiss him, and are now carrying on their phony campaign. This deceives nobody who knows them.

In 1929 it was the policy of Moscow to carry on a vicious campaign against all capitalists and every section of the labor movement which was not Stalinist. That was their notorious "third period." In accordance with this line, they were prepared to make the film exposing American capitalism. As soon, however, as the capitalists gave any indication that they opposed it, the Moscow bureaucrats, as usual, capitulated. In 1934, on the other hand, they began their new policy of support to the "democracies" against the fascist imperialists. During this campaign, behind all their noisy talk, they capitulated on every front to what they called the "democratic forces." Roosevelt was their hero, Eleanor Roosevelt their heroine, and their chief care was to penetrate as far as possible into those elements of "democracy" which they thought might be useful in furthering the alliance between America and Russia. They shoved the Negro movement as far as possible into the Negro National Congress.

With the Hitler-Stalin pact this "fourth period" came to an end. Stalin now wishes them to build as much opposition as possible in the camp of the "democracies" in order to assist the victory of the Hitler-Stalin camp. Therefore they rediscover the revolutionary instincts of the Negro people; they begin a great drive in Harlem. And they tear their hair and gnash their teeth at the crimes of *Gone With the Wind*.

To conclude, the film is dangerous and must be exposed and boycotted. But infinitely more dangerous, and therefore to be exposed and boycotted to an infinitely greater degree, is this mischievous manipulation of Negro militancy in the interest of the Moscow bureaucrats.

On *Native Son* by Richard Wright (1940)

Six weeks after publication, *Native Son*, a novel about a Negro by a Negro, Richard Wright, had sold a quarter of a million copies. This is not only a question of literature. Whatever brings a nationally oppressed minority to the notice of the oppressing majority is of political importance.

Bigger Thomas, the hero, comes very close to raping a white woman; then, accidentally, it is true, murders her. He burns the corpse in the furnace.

Then he writes a fake kidnapper's note, demanding ten thousand dollars as the price of restoring her to her home. His crime is discovered and to save himself he cold-bloodedly kills his Negro girl-friend, Bessie. He is caught and is sentenced to death. The action takes place in Chicago.

Crime and the Negro

This is the bald outline of the story, and periodically you can read in the press similar stories about Negro "rapists" and Negro "killers." Not only the white but the Negro press features such crimes. Whenever the Anti-Lynching Bill comes up in the House you can be sure to hear Southern Senators quoting statistics to show the high percentage of dangerous criminals in the Negro population.

Now, the most dangerous criminals, gangsters and racketters in America are not Negroes. Al Capone is no Negro. But Richard Wright, the Negro author, has accepted the challenge. He says in effect, "You fill your press with accounts of Negro crime. In the South, you use the Negro's alleged criminality to prove that he can only be kept in order by extra-legal means, such as lynching and brutal segregation. Very well then, let us take one of the worst possible examples of Negro crime; let us examine the case; let us see who this criminal is; let us see whom he murdered and why; let us see what was his state of mind before he murdered and after. Let us see who were his friends, who persecuted him, who tried to help him before the murders, and who tried to help him afterwards."

The result is one of the most powerful novels of the last twenty-five years. Wright says: Black Bigger did the things he did because American capitalist society has made an outcast of the black man. Bigger is not the sinner. He is the man sinned against. Bigger stands in the dock and is sentenced but it is the American social order which is on trial.

To conceive such an idea and to carry it out as Wright has done is a tremendous achivement.

Is Bigger "Typical"?

People have criticized Bigger Thomas as not being a "typical" Negro. What is a "typical" Negro? "Typical" of what? In capitalist society at the present time, no "typical" Negro could express the point of view that Wright wished to portray. Bigger Thomas represents the Negro in revolt. He does not quote Marx and say, "Workers of the world unite," or, "Black and white, unite and fight." He does not even know what the "Reds" stand for. But he is a revolutionary nevertheless, instinctive but none the less powerful. In his eyes, as in the eyes of most Negroes, it is white society which suppresses him, humiliates him, stands over him with a whip and keeps him cowering in holes and corners.

And Bigger will not stand for it. He hates the white skin as the obvious symbol of his oppression. It is an accident which sets him off on his career. It is his intense nature which drives him so far along the path of crime. But in his sense of oppression, his hatred of the whites, and his violence, once he takes that road, he is typical of millions of Negroes.

The great majority of them feel as Bigger feels, think as Bigger thinks, and hate as Bigger hates; but they have learnt to suppress it. The flames burn very low, but they are there. Far more powerful stimuli will be needed to make them act as Bigger acted. That is all.

When Liebnicht said in 1914, "The main enemy is a home," he seemed a lone figure, a madman. But by November 1918 he was a very "typical" German. In that all important sense Bigger is "typical." He is not travelling up a by-path. He is on the main road, only further on than the rest of his people. A great social crisis will convert millions of Negroes into Bigger Thomases. Only where he acted against isolated persons, they will act against organized society.

A Novel that Approaches Greatness

Wright shows all but the most supreme confidence in the rightness of his theme and his capacity to carry it out. I say "all but," because Wright makes Bigger very nearly rape the woman and commit the first murder by accident, at least as far as he acted consciously. Shakespeare and Dostoevsky certainly, and perhaps Tolstoy, would not have hesitated; they would have made Bigger consciously commit both crimes. That Wright was not certain of himself is proved by the fact, among others, that he makes a lawyer deliver a long, bad, and tiresome speech at the very end of the book, saying all over again what the book had already very clearly and powerfully said. He need not have been afraid. The novel contains abundant evidence that he could have carried even this extension of his theme to a triumphant success.

Consider, for example, the main psychological theme of the book. Bigger commits murder. But having committed murder, in the instinct to save himself, he pits his brains against the whites and for the first time is conscious of acting as a man, free, unrestricted, and with a will of his own. Wright does not only say this in words. He has conceived and executed his novel in those terms. Before the murder Bigger is irresolute, frustrated, longing but hopeless. Once he realizes, however, that he has committed murder and must defend himself, he becomes the embodiment of initiative, endurance, courage, and will. How the boy fights! I can remember nowhere in literature so magnificent and yet so unrhetorical a determination to fight to the end. It is not merely for his life. Trapped on the roof, he counts his bullets and leaves the last one for himself. It is pride in himself, as a free man with a hardly-bought freedom. He will not capitulate to those white men—it is revolutionary pride.

PUBLIC AWARENESS OF THE NEGRO QUESTION (1945)

The press in recent days has been filled with reviews praising *Black Boy*, a book by Richard Wright, the author of *Native Son*, a novel which had an enormous circulation some years ago. The new work is an autobiography, a record of Wright's Negro childhood and youth in the South.

It is not my purpose to review the book here, except to say that it is, in my humble opinion, a successful attempt to portray in terms of an individual life what living in America means to a modern Negro. On the jacket, Bennett Cerf, a critic, is quoted as saying of the book: "Beautifully written, with the impact of a battleship." It is the impact with which I am here concerned. For this impact is in reality the impact of a tenth of a nation upon the contemporary American consciousness.

In 1944, another book that dealt with the Negro question made, in its own way, an effective impact upon the United States. It was called *Strange Fruit*. Written by a Southern white woman of liberal ideas, Lillian Smith, it dealt seriously and honestly with race relations in the South. Hundreds of thousands of copies were sold.

Toward the end of 1943 the scientific and sociological world, and not they alone, were startled by two splendid volumes, entitled *An American Dilemma*. The dilemma was the Negro question. The history of this book is significant, especially for labor. It was a serious scientific study, taking years of research and organization. Every accepted writer, every economist, every sociologist, white and Negro, who had knowledge or ideas, was invited to cooperate. This took money and the money, some quarter of a million dollars, came from the Carnegie Endowment Fund. In other words, big capital paid for it.

The choice of an investigator to coordinate the material was also striking. It said openly that it could not trust an American, however able and however honest, because the deeply ingrained and traditional racial prejudices of the United States would affect his judgement. This does not mean that necessarily the writer would be anti-Negro. He might try *not* to be anti-Negro, but this too would not be conducive to scientific accuracy. The capitalists wanted the facts. (What it would do with them was its own business.) For the same reason, the Carnegie Fund said it did not want an Englishman or any European from the imperialist countries. It therefore chose a Swede, Gunnar Myrdal.

The book was very large and cost $7.50 a copy. It was not intended, obviously, for the general public. To the surprise of many, despite its solid treatment of the subject and the all-but-prohibitive price, it was a popular success. The first edition disappeared. It is being widely read today.

Still another novel recently published, *Freedom Road* by Howard Fast, has made its impact upon the reading public. It deals with the Negroes in the Reconstruction period. It is selling well and is widely discussed.

Now, all this is not accidental. It is a sign of the times. Why should talented writers choose these subjects? Why should they write so well about them? Why should the general public grasp at them so eagerly? It is because they are a manifestation of the social crisis in the United States. As the contradictions of capitalism in the United States multiply and sharpen they bring to the fore all the sores inherent in a rotting society.

The major problem of capitalism in general is unemployment. The books, the solutions, the arguments on it pour down upon us. But in every country capitalism has special problems. In the United States such a special problem is the Negro question. Hence the presentation of it from so many different points of view, and the enthusiastic response of the public.

But literature is only one phase of this crisis. The other is more important. The public has not been stimulated only by ideas and by an intellectual interest in the problems of the day. The Negroes themselves in the March on Washington agitation, and in their violent protests in Detroit and Harlem, have made the American people aware of them and their resentment.

In its struggles with rival imperialisms, American imperialism itself has been compelled to drag hundreds of Negroes into the production process. Thereby organized labor has been brought sharply up against the Negro question, and the CIO has taken vigorous action to incorporate Negroes into its own ranks on terms of equality.

The books and their millions of readers, the actions of the Negroes, the organizational response of labor, can be termed as, on the whole, overwhelmingly progressive. The general tendency of ideas and actions is toward abolition of the oppression and humiliation of Negroes. Even the book the capitalists financed expressed itself (in wishy-washy terms) as aiming at some solution of the dilemma in terms of the Negro's incorporation into American society on equal terms. The others make no bones about the necessity of this. And the public that reads them so eagerly is obviously in sympathy. That is splendid.

To state a problem in harshly truthful and moving terms is fine; for millions to read eagerly about it and be sympathetic about its solution is also fine. Also wherever there is such strong public feeling there is always a will to action. For the will to action, like the books and the readers, is also a manifestation of the social crisis. The question is what to do. And here the trouble begins.

If the facts we have observed are the expression of the social crisis, then the solution, the ideas of solution, must penetrate to the very essence of the social problem—that is to say, to the nature of capitalist society itself. For if not, there is nothing in store but disappointment, disillusionment, and despair.

An old proverb says that desperate diseases demand desperate remedies. The readers of books, the protesting Negro masses, the labor unions striving for social solidarity, the collective will to action which is maturing and achieving results in the labor movement—these varying forces will not be able to avoid the ultimate answer: capitalism or socialism.

JOE LOUIS AND JACK JOHNSON (1946)

A tense political or social situation can take the simplest or most commonplace event and make it into a symbol of political struggle. The most famous of such cases is the Dreyfus case in France fifty years ago. Lenin once pointed out how this anti-Semitic attack by the military caste on a Jewish officer nearly precipitated a revolution in France.

The situation of the Negroes has in the past lifted sporting events in which Negroes took part to a level of international political interest. Observers in

Europe in 1935 noted the great satisfaction with which "the left" greeted the Olympic victories of the American Negroes. These games took place in Berlin, under Hitler's very nose. His obnoxious racial theories were debunked on the presence of thousands of fanatical Nazis.

Now Joe Louis retains his title as heavyweight champion of the world. The Negroes rejoice, and the labor movement should view with sympathy and understanding their deep satisfaction. The Negroes express by this a very simple, very human, and for that reason, social sentiment of great significance. "Negroes are inferior? Very well then. Here is one Negro who is not inferior and beats everybody who dares to challenge him."

The British government with its long experience in colonial domination, allows no nonsense of that kind. It prohibits by law competition for boxing titles between Englishmen and colored colonials, and we need have no doubt that if the reactionaries in the U.S. ever got their chance they would restrict the championship to whites only. Luckily, the labor movement (whether individual workers supported Louis or Conn) would raise such a howl, that these fascistic types would have to keep their mouths shut.

Joe Louis, however, is a remarkable person, and has stamped his personality on this generation. He is a man of great personal dignity, and has borne the temptations and the publicity associated with the championship in a manner that has won the admiration of all. This has led to comments on Louis as a "representative of his race"—the announcer on the night of the big fight referred to him as such.

Jimmy Cannon of the *New York Post* wrote a column which ended with the phrase that Joe was a credit to his race. But he added immediately, "I mean the human race." Harlem was vastly pleased with this and the phrase has acquired wings among the Negro people.

At the opposite extreme is the *New York Times*. A few days before the fight Jack Johnson, another Negro champion, died. Johnson had had a stormy and spectacular career and had served time in prison. The *Times* said in so many words that Johnson's conduct had cast a stain upon the Negro character which Louis's conduct was wiping away. This is a piece of ignorance and impertinence which deserves to be exposed.

Jack Johnson was champion of the old school of champions. In those days, the days of John L. Sullivan, J. J. Corbett, etc, the champions lived fast. What made the authorities mad was that Johnson refused to act differently simply because he was a Negro. He insisted on his right to live his own way. He was persecuted but remained irrepressible to the end. Doubtless he did many wrong and stupid things. But Negro publicists who followed his career have denounced all attempts to make him into a kind of Negro black sheep.

Similarly this attempt to hold up Louis as a model Negro has strong overtones of condescension and race prejudice. It implies: "See! When a Negro knows how to conduct himself, he gets on very well and we all love him." From there the next step is: "If only all Negroes behaved like Joe, the race problem would be solved."

And yet there *is* a sense in which the careful public conduct of Joe Louis is a matter not only of his personal character but of his origin. Joe himself has stated in public that he would rather die than do anything which would discredit his people. In this he reflects the acute social consciousness of the generation to which he belongs. The Negro question today is not what it was in Jack Johnson's time. Joe feels that he is not only a boxer but a social figure, someone whose actions can harm the struggle of Negroes for their full democratic rights. In that sense he feels he is a genuine "representative" of the Negro people. He feels it strongly and the Negroes, recognizing this, admire him for it as well as for his boxing prowess. That is not only legitimate but is good and in its way progressive. To the Negroes, it is only another reason why they should not be deprived of their rights. The important thing is to separate this healthy sentiment from the smug and hypocritical who clasp their hands across their chests and whine: "If only Negroes conducted themselves like Joe Louis, the Negro problem would be solved."

FOUR

Towards a Synthesis

THE HISTORICAL DEVELOPMENT OF THE NEGROES IN AMERICAN SOCIETY (1943)

The history of the Negro question and the American revolutionary movement in general, and the Trotskyist movement in particular, makes it imperative at this stage to outline in however brief a form the role of the Negroes in the political development of American society.

In 1776 the masses of the Negroes played no initiatory role and the revolution would have taken the general course it did if not one single Negro lived in the United States. However, as soon as the actual revolutionary struggle began, the Negroes compelled the revolutionary bourgeoisie to include the rights of Negroes among the rights of man. The Negroes themselves played a powerful part in the military struggle of the revolution.

Between 1800 and 1830 the Negroes, disappointed in the results of the revolution, staged a continuous series of revolts. By 1831 the petty-bourgeois democracy of the United States entered upon a period of widespread egalitarian and humanitarian agitation. Disappointed by their failures between 1800 and 1830, the Negro slaves in the South, aided by free Negroes in the North, sought their freedom by mass flight. Owing to this spontaneous action, the petty-bourgeois movement for the rights of the common man was soon dominated by the struggle for the abolition of slavery. The link between the Northern bourgeoisie and the Southern planters was far stronger by 1860 than the link between the colonial bourgeoisie and the British in 1776. The Northern bourgeoisie used all possible means to avoid the revolutionary clash. The most powerful subjective influence which forced the irrepressibility of the conflict upon the consciousness of the people was the agitation of the petty-bourgeoisie, stimulated, maintained, and intensified over the years by the refusal of the masses of slaves to accept their position. In the course of the Civil War the revolutionary actions of the masses of the Negroes in the South played a decisive role in the winning of the Northern victory.

In the agrarian movement of the 1890s in the South the Negro farmers and semi-proletarians, independently organized to the extent of a million and a quarter members in the National Colored Farmers Alliance, were a militant and powerful wing of the Populist movement. They supported the break with the Republican Party and the proposal for a third party with social as well as economic aims.

The importance of the Negroes as a revolutionary force has grown with the development of the American economy. Conversely, however, racial prejudice against the Negroes has also grown. Between 1830 and 1860 the Southern planters cultivated the theory of Negro inferiority to a degree far exceeding that of earlier slavery days, being driven to do this by the increasing divergences between the developing bourgeois democracy in the United States and the needs of the slave economy. To conquer the formidable threat of white and Negro unity, particularly that represented by Populism, the Southern plantocracy elevated race consciousness to the position of a principle. The whole country was injected with this idea. Thus, side by side with his increasing *integration* into production which becomes more and more a social process, the Negro becomes more than ever conscious of his *exclusion* from democratic privileges as a separate social group in the community. *This dual movement is the key to the Marxist analysis of the Negro question in the U.S.A.*

At the same time in the country as a whole, as in the world at large, the rights of democracy become more and more a burning political question in view of the widespread attack by declining bourgeois society upon the principles of democracy in general. Simultaneously, the rise of the labor movement brings increasing consciousness of labor as a social force in the reorganization of society. Thus the Negro in his century and a half old struggle for democratic rights is increasingly confronted with the subjective consciousness of himself as an oppressed racial minority and the objective consciousness of labor as the great bulwark of democracy in the country at large.

It is in the light of this contradiction that we must trace the development among Negroes of the sense of nationalistic oppression and the modern efforts to free themselves from it.

Negro Nationalism: First Phase

The first reaction of the masses of the Negroes to the consolidation of the Solid South was the policy of Booker T. Washington, who counselled submission, industrial training, and the development of Negro business. For the moment the Negroes in the South seemed to acquiesce. But in reality there grew up a furious but suppressed hatred of whites at the oppression and particularly at the racial humiliation to which Negroes were now being subjected. *The appreciation of this is fundamental to any understanding of the Negro question.*

During World War I the needs of Northern industry brought a million Negroes to the North. The suppressed resentment burst out and was organized and mislead as Garveyism. Thus when this essentially nationalistic explosion took place immediately the Negroes gained some integration into American society which allowed them free expression. Its first significance was the indication that it gave of the powerful force of social protest which smoldered in the hearts of the Negroes. Its second is the fact that it took place precisely because the Negro had made economic and social progress.

The Negro and Organized Labor

The Negroes, due to their place as the most oppressed section of the labor force and their sense of national oppression, have always shown themselves on the whole exceptionally ready to join the forces of organized labor. The exclusion of Negroes from the AFL corresponded to a period of class collaboration practiced by the AFL leadership. When the Industrial Workers of the World (IWW) raised the banner of militant trade unionism among the most oppressed and exploited sections of the working population, Negro labor responded both as rank and filers and as good organizers. Moreover, the IWW gave the Negroes the sense of a social program for the regeneration of society to which also the Negroes have always been responsive.

In 1932 the Negroes, like the rest of the labor movement, followed the New Deal program with its vast promises of a new order in America. But the Roosevelt government, while of necessity including the Negroes in its social service program for the unemployed, did nothing to implement its vague promises for the amelioration of the national oppression of Negroes in the country.

The CIO, being mainly an organization of the heavy industries, was compelled to organize the Negroes in great industries like steel and auto or face the impossibility of any organization at all. The Negro masses, despite some hesitation, responded magnificently and today they constitute powerful and progressive groups in many unions of the CIO.

This entry into the militant trade-union movement is undoubtedly of great significance not only for organized labor as a whole but for the Negro people. Yet the main struggle of the Negro masses in the United States has been and until the achievement of socialism will continue to be their struggle for their democratic rights as a nationally oppressed minority. Their entry into the ranks of organized labor does not lessen their sense of national oppression. On the contrary, it increases it and, in full accordance with their role in past American revolutionary crises and the developing antagonisms of American society, this independent action of the Negro masses is already playing a role in relation to the American proletariat which constitutes one of the most important elements in the struggle for socialism.

Negro Nationalism: Second Phase
The tumultuous world situation, the loud-voiced shrieking of "democracy" by Anglo-American imperialism and the increasing demands of organized labor in America for greater and greater extensions of its democratic rights, stimulated in the Negro people by the beginning of World War II a more than usually intensive desire to struggle for equality. Driven by the necessities of war, the Roosevelt government called upon the people of America to make the greater sacrifices necessary for war in the name of democracy. At the same time, however, the special needs and practices of Southern society and industry as a whole, fortified by the now deeply-ingrained race prejudice of American society, prohibited any extension of democracy to the Negro people. Instead the persecution and discrimination of World War I have been intensified. The violent attacks and humiliations to which the Negro people have been subjected, in the Army in particular, have raised the indignation of the Negro masses to a high pitch.

The Negroes have responded with a nation-wide offensive. This offensive, which especially sought the right of entry into industry and also into

Jim Crow unions, has expressed itself not only in mass movements but in a growing determination to struggle in an individual and often terroristic manner against any manifestation of white superiority. The younger Negroes in particular now walk the streets in many towns determined to assert themselves. And in states like Virginia, the Carolinas, and Tennessee their attitude in street cars, their resentful submission to the old Jim Crow laws, have created a degree of social tension unknown in those parts for two generations. This has been one of the main contributing causes to the series of racial outbreaks which have taken place in various parts of the country. The Attorney General of the United States has made the fantastic and unprecedented proposal to prohibit the Negroes from coming into Northern cities and has publicly expressed his fears of imminent race riots. He thus typifies the bankruptcy of the bourgeoisie in the face of the mass offensive of the Negroes.

The character and high state of development of the nation-wide Negro offensive is best typified by its expression in Harlem. Harlem is the largest urban concentration of Negroes in the country. It is the area in which Negroes feel safest, freest, and therefore most able to express their resentment. It is therefore precisely in Harlem that appear most powerfully the nationalistic sentiments of the Negro and the deepest social protests. In 1935 the Negroes in Harlem carried out a spontaneous demonstration against their general social conditions and particularly against the non-employment of Negroes in Harlem stores. The demonstrations initiated a movement which has made substantial corrections of this injustice. In 1941 the Harlem community organized and carried to success a demonstration against the non-employment of bus-drivers. Similar actions or attempts at action have taken place all over the country, except in the very deep South.

The Negroes have not been satisfied with local or merely regional demonstrations. Highly significant is the organized expression of their boiling resentment. As far back as 1940, Councilman Powell, realizing the need for giving some national organized expression to this widespread resentment, tried to summon a national conference of Negro leaders in New York. The movement did not materialize, but by 1941 the pressure of the Negro masses had forced the formation of an organization aimed at marching on Washington and making a forcible protest to the state against the national oppression of the Negroes.

The Negro petty-bourgeois leaders found their organization in the NAACP and the Urban league rejected by the Negro masses as unsuitable for their militant purposes. They trembled before this powerful urge of the Negro masses to confront the capitalist state with a comprehensive protest against their grievances. In the persons of A. Philip Randolph and Walter White they rushed to head the movement and immediately turned it over to the Roosevelt government which transformed itself into leader of the Negro people under the guise of the FEPC. The Negro masses waited patiently upon the FEPC to solve their problems in industry and upon the capitalist state to improve the situation of Negroes in the Army. With the failure of the Roosevelt government and the FEPC to ameliorate their grievances, the masses of the Negro people arrived at the decision that they must take matters into their own hands. The most outstanding expression of this sentiment was the Harlem demonstration, participated in by many thousands of people, viewed sympathetically by the large majority of the people of Harlem and Negroes all over the United States. When examined in its totality it will be seen as one of the most significant manifestations of independent social protest among Negroes that has taken place since the Garvey movement. This is no question merely of bad housing, insufficient playgrounds, or increasing poverty.

The Harlem demonstration, like the miners' strike, represents a significant stage in the development of the struggle against capitalist society. The miners' strike was an indication not only of the immediate grievances of the miners but of the stage of development reached by the American proletariat as a whole. The miners did what millions of Americans wanted to do. The Harlem action is equally an indication of the sentiments of the great majority of the Negroes in this country. Both of these manifestations in their strength and in their weaknesses are the two most important indications of the developing mass resentment against the existing, i.e., the capitalist, society that have resulted from the strain of the war.

At the same time the petty-bourgeois leaders among the Negroes have issued a political manifesto which, despite all its weaknesses, show that the Negro people as a whole have reached the stage of taking a critical attitude, as Negroes, to both the Democratic and Republican parties. Both the Negroes protesting in the streets and the timid and vacillating petty-bourgeois have now reached a stage in their evolution where, as always in the their past history, their next historic step is toward unity with the revolutionary class, in our day, the American proletariat. *To the degree that the Negroes are more integrated into industry and unions their consciousness of racial oppression and their resentment against it become heavier, not less.* This dual development of the Negro people during the last few years poses exceptional problems and exceptional opportunities for the American proletariat and therefore for the revolutionary party.

The American Proletariat and the Negro Question Today

The American proletariat is the class whose objective role at the present stage is to solve the fundamental problems of American society. Any *theoretical* analysis of the contemporary Negro problem must therefore begin with the developing relation of the Negro struggle to the general struggles of the proletariat as the leader of the oppressed classes in American society.

i. In the present stage of American capitalism the great danger threatening the masses of the people is fascism. Events in Detroit and elsewhere have shown that the fascistic elements will exploit to the limit the Negro problem in the United States to confuse, disorganize, and divide the great masses of the people and to disrupt their natural leader in the struggle against Fascism, the organized force of labor.

ii. The American bourgeoisie, whether Democratic or Republican, is perfectly aware of the permanent nature of the agricultural crisis and has already shown its determination to bribe the farmers to support it against organized labor. However, the problems of the poor farmers, the tenant farmers, the sharecroppers, and the agricultural proletariat are insoluble in capitalist society. The solution of the agrarian problem in the United States rests with the proletariat and any solution involves automatically the general *social situation* of millions of Negroes in the Southern states.

iii. The South presents the gravest problem of democracy in the United States. Economic remnants of slavery, a large landless peasantry, the development of large-scale and, especially, the extractive industries, the transference of textile industry from the North, a developing labor movement—all these are permeated with a caste system comparable to nothing else in the modern world. Holding together these diverse and contradictory elements is a political superstructure with the external forms of bourgeois democracy. This extraordinary conglomeration of explosive forces is situated not as in India, thousands of miles away from the metropolis, but in the very heart of the most advanced political bourgeois democracy in the world.

Armed with Trotsky's theory of the permanent revolution, which we must apply at home as well as abroad, the Bolshevik party must be able to foresee the telescoping of the industrial, agricultural, and social revolution in the South. These contradictions are developing at a time when Fascism, the enemy of democracy and the most outspoken of all proponents of racial domination, is experiencing signal defeats administered at the cost of great sacrifices to the American people. The gross hypocrisy involved has made deep penetration into the minds of Negroes in the South. Familiarity with that situation and the comparative acceptance by the masses, particularly the Negro masses, in the past, should not dull our comprehension of the potential dynamite which the situation represents.

It is possible that before the general economic and political forces in the South have reached the point of explosion, the Negro masses may by independent mass actions pose all questions purely in terms of equality of Negro rights. Whatever the pace of the general development or the forms that it may take, we must expect that in the course of the next period, the period of the social crisis in America, the American proletariat as a whole will be faced with this problem.

iv. Even today, in the day-to-day struggles for democratic rights, the Southern landlords and industrialists have proved themselves the unyielding enemies, not only of the working class but of the democratic rights of the whole American people. Large sections of American society, particularly organized labor and the great number of Negroes in the North are now fully aware of this and are aware also that the basis of Southern political power is the economic and social degradation of the Negroes in the South.

From the above four points, certain conclusions of extreme importance to the American proletariat can be drawn. In America as in every other country, the basic struggle is between the proletariat and the bourgeoisie for the control of the economic sources of social and political power. But in every country this struggle assumes special historical forms. It is the task of the revolutionary party first of all to clarify itself in order to be able to clarify the proletariat on the crucial role of the Negro problem in the defense of its own position and the socialist reconstruction of American society.

The Negro Question as a National Question

The 14 million Negroes in the United States are subjected to every conceivable variety of economic oppression and social and political discrimination. These tortures are to a degree sanctified by law and practiced without shame by all the organs of government. The Negroes, however, are and have been for many centuries in every sense of the word, Americans. They are not separated from their oppressors by differences of culture, differences of religion, differences of language, as the inhabitants of India or Africa. They are not even regionally separated from the rest of the community as national groups in Russia, Spain, or Yugoslavia.

The Negroes are for the most part proletarian or semi-proletarian and therefore the struggle of the Negroes is fundamentally a class question.

The Negroes do not constitute a nation, but, owing to their special situation, their segregation; economic, social, and political oppression; the difference in color which singles them out so easily from the rest of the community; their problems become the problem of a national minority. The Negro question is a part of the national and not of the "national" question. This national minority is most easily distinguished from the rest of the community by its racial characteristics. Thus the Negro question is a question of race and not of "race."

The contrasts between their situation and the privileges enjoyed by those around them have always made the Negroes that section of American society most receptive to revolutionary ideas and the radical solution of social problems. The white working class struggles against the objective rule of capital and for some subjective goal, which even on the very eve of revolution, is impossible to visualize fully in concrete and positive terms. The Negroes, on the other hand, struggle and will continue to struggle objectively against capital, but in contrast to the white workers, for the very concrete objective democratic rights that they see around them.

But the whole history of the United States and the role of the Negroes in American economy and society are a constant proof and reminder of the fact that it is absolutely impossible for the Negroes to gain equality under American capitalism.

Such is the development of American capitalist society and the role of Negroes in it that the Negroes' struggle for democratic rights brings the Negroes almost immediately face to face with capital and the state. *The Marxist support of the Negro struggle for democratic rights is not a concession that Marxists make to the Negroes. In the United States today this struggle is a direct part of the struggle for socialism.*

National Struggle and the Struggle for Socialism

All serious problems arising from the Negro question revolve around the relationship of the independent mass actions of the Negroes for democratic rights to the working class struggle for socialism.

In the Second Congress of the Communist International, Lenin's theses singled out as examples of the national and colonial question the Irish question and the question of the Negroes in America. This Leninist approach was based upon close study of the economic situation of the Negroes in the United States and the Irish Rebellion in 1916. The whole historical development of the Negro struggle in the United States and its relations to the social struggles of the revolutionary classes show that the Leninist analysis of the Negro question as part of the national question is the correct method with which to approach this problem. It is necessary, therefore, to have a precise and clear conception of the application of this *method*. The most concentrated example of it is Lenin's treatment of the Irish Rebellion during World War I.

Lenin wishes to illustrate the specifically *nationalist* struggle of the Irish Rebellion in its relation to the *socialist* struggle of the British proletariat against British imperialism. He uses the experience of the Russian Revolution in 1905 which took place exclusively *within the national boundaries of Russia*. He uses also, *not* the struggles of the nationally oppressed minorities, but the struggles of the petty-bourgeoisie, the peasants and other non-proletarian, non-class groups, in relation to the struggle of the Russian proletariat. We have therefore a very concrete illustration of the applicability of the method to environments and classes superficially diverse but organically similar.

(a) "The Russian Revolution of 1905 was a bourgeois-democratic revolution. It consisted of a series of battles in which all the discontented classes, groups, and elements of the population participated. Among these were masses imbued with the crudest prejudices, with the vaguest and most fantastic aims of struggle; there were small groups which accepted Japanese money, there were speculators and adventurers, etc. *Objectively*, the mass movement broke the back of tsarism and paved the way for democracy; for that reason the class-conscious workers led it."

Within the United States the socialist revolution will ultimately consist of a series of battles in which the discontented classes, groups and elements of all types will participate in their own way and form a contributory force to the great culminating struggles which will be led by the proletariat.

(b) "The socialist revolution in Europe *cannot be anything else* than an outburst of mass struggle on the part of all and sundry of the oppressed and discontented elements. Sections of the petty bourgeoisie and of the backward workers will inevitably participate in it—without such participation, *mass struggle is impossible*, without it *no revolution* is possible—and just as inevitably will they bring into the movement their weaknesses and errors. But *objectively* they will attack *capital* and the class-conscious vanguard of the revolution, the advanced proletariat, expressing this objective truth of a heterogeneous and discordant, motley, and outwardly incohesive mass struggle will be able to unite and direct it, to capture power, to seize the banks, to expropriate the trusts, hated by all, though for different reasons. . . ."

In the United States social revolution is impossible without the independent mass struggles of the Negroes, whatever the prejudices, the reactionary fantasies, the weaknesses and errors of these struggles. The proletarian composition of the Negro people and the developing labor movement, offer great opportunities for a continuous reduction of the prejudices of the Negro people.

(c) "The struggle of the oppressed nations IN EUROPE, a struggle capable of going to the lengths of insurrection and street fighting, of breaking down the iron discipline in the army and martial law, will 'sharpen the revolutionary crisis in Europe' infinitely more than a much more developed rebellion in a remote colony. A blow delivered against the English imperialist bourgeoisie by a rebellion in Ireland is a hundred times more significant politically than a blow of equal weight delivered in Asia or Africa."

Blows delivered by an oppressed national minority so entangled in the social structure of the United States as the Negroes, possess a political significance of greater importance in this country than a blow delivered by any other section of the population except the organized proletariat itself.

(d) "The dialectics of history is such that small nations, powerless as an INDEPENDENT factor in the struggle against imperialism, play a part as one of the ferments, one of the bacilli, which help the REAL power against imperialism to come on the scene, namely the SOCIALIST PROLETARIAT."

Within the United States, the Negroes are undoubtedly powerless to achieve their complete or even substantial emancipation as an independent factor in the struggle against American capital but such is the historic role of the Negroes in the United States; such today is their proletarian composition and such is the interrelation with the American proletariat itself that their independent struggles form perhaps the most powerful stimulus in American society to the recognition by the organized proletariat of its real responsibilities to the national development as a whole and of its power against American imperialism.

The ideal situation is that the struggle of the minority group should be organized and led by the proletariat. But to make this a precondition of supporting the struggle of non-proletarian, semi-proletarian, or non-class conscious groups is a repudiation of all Marxist theory and practice. *Thus it is utterly false to draw the conclusion that the independent struggle of the Negro masses for their democratic rights is to be looked upon merely as a preliminary stage to a recognition by the Negroes that the real struggle is the struggle for socialism.*

The Marxist Movement and the Negro Question

The Marxist movement in the United States with little exception has failed to grasp the fact that the Negro question is part of the national question. This is not surprising because it has shown little interest in the Negroes except under the direct and insistent stimulus of the internationalist movement.

The socialist movement under Debs considered any special appeal to the Negro people as contrary to the spirit of socialism. Randolph appealed to Negroes to become socialists but proved quite incapable of dealing with the powerful nationalistic current of Garveyism that was prevalent at the time. The Communist Party up to 1928 was unable to understand either the significance of the Negro question in the U.S. or the method of work required. It was only through the drastic intervention of the Communist International, whatever its purpose, that the Communist Party in 1929 began a serious approach to the Negro question. Despite many exaggerations, the turn to the Negro question was on the whole sound and effective, but it was seriously handicapped by the adoption of a policy of advocating self-determination for the Black Belt. In 1935 with the new turn of the Communist International toward social patriotism, the work of the Communist Party among Negroes began a process of rapid deterioration. The Trotskyist movement from its foundation in 1928 to 1938 took even less interest in the Negro question than the Communist Party and once more it was only under the insistence of the international organization that the American Marxist movement took action on the Negro question.

Trotsky and the Negro Question

Trotsky began to take a special interest in the Negro question as soon as he applied himself to the problems of the United States from the point of view of building a Trotskyist revolutionary organization. From that time he never ceased to point out the importance of this question. Though scattered and to some degree incidental, his conversations and discussions are organized by a consistent approach and, altogether, constitute a remarkable example of Marxist penetration into the correct basis for any Negro work in the U.S. In any resolution on the Negro question at this stage, it is necessary to summarize briefly his ideas.

On the question of self-determination, Trotsky believed that the differences between the West Indies, Catalonia, Poland, etc. and the situation of the Negroes in the United States were not decisive. In other words, the Negro question was a part of the national question. He firmly opposed those in the Fourth International who rejected outright the principle of self-determination for Negroes in the U.S. In a discussion in 1939 he made it clear that he did not propose that the party advocate the slogan of self-determination for Negroes in the U.S. but he insisted that the party should declare its obligation to struggle with the Negroes for self-determination, should they at any time demand it. Trotsky insisted that if the Negroes should decide, under the stress of unforseen historical events (e.g., a period of Fascism in the U.S.), to struggle for self-determination, the struggle would under all circumstances be progressive, for the simple reason that it could not possibly be attained except through war against American capitalism.

Trotsky's views on the Negro question are most clearly, though not completely, contained in a discussion in 1939. In his approach to Negro work, Trotsky based his views on the sentiments of the genuine Negro masses in the U.S. and the fact that their oppression as Negroes was so strong that they feel it at every moment.

Of those suffering from oppression and discrimination, the Negroes were the most oppressed and the most discriminated against and therefore formed part of the most dynamic milieu of the working class. The party should say to the conscious elements among the Negroes that they have been convoked by the historical development to take their place in the very vanguard of the working class struggle for socialism. Trotsky considered that if the party was unable to find a road to this stratum of society, in which he gave the Negroes a very important place, then it would be a confession of revolutionary futility.

While conscious of the role of the Negro in the vanguard, however, Trotsky placed a heavy emphasis always on the consciousness of Negroes as being a nationally oppressed minority. On every possible occasion he emphasized the political conclusions that were to be drawn from the social situation of the Negroes under American capitalism for 300 years. He warned repeatedly of the probability of violent racial outbreaks among the Negroes in which they would seek to revenge themselves for all the oppression and humiliations which they had suffered.

Trotsky took the greatest interest in the Garvey movement as an expression of the genuine sentiments of the Negro masses who were always his main concern. He constantly recommended to the party the study of the Negroes in the Civil War as a historical necessity for understanding the Negro question today. He recommended the study of Garvey's movement as an indispensable indication to the party of the road to the Negro masses. He welcomed the idea of an independent mass organization of the Negro people, formed through the instrumentality of the party. His general approach to the Negro question can best be indicated by the following fact: he recommended that under certain circumstances the revolutionary party should withdraw its own candidate for election to Congress and support a Negro Democrat put forward by a Negro community anxious to have its own Negro representative. In all these ideas Trotsky merely exemplified the application to the concrete struggle of the original principle embodied in the right to self-determination.

No task is more urgent than the collation and publication of Trotsky's writings and ideas on the Negro question in the U.S., their close study by all members of the party, and their dissemination in an organized form among the proletariat and the Negro masses.

Part II: The Workers Party and the Negro Question

The problem of the party therefore divides itself into two parts: (1) the struggle of the American proletariat for socialism and its relation to the Negro struggle for democratic rights; and (2) the independent struggles of the Negroes for democratic rights and its relation to the proletarian struggle for socialism. Under no circumstances are these separate elements to be confused or treated as one.

The Workers Party and Negro Work in the Organized Labor Movement

The Workers Party approaches Negro work in the organized labor movement from the basis of the approaching social crisis, and the preparation of the proletariat for the socialist revolution. Today one of the greatest subjective weaknesses of the American proletariat is the absence of consciousness that labor is opposed to capital for leadership of the nation. This being so, it follows that the other oppressed and discontented classes, elements, and groups have not yet learned to look to labor for a partial or even a "reformist" solution to their problem. Classes learn such lessons only by massive experiences on a national scale; only in the very last stages of the revolution did the Russian peasantry learn that the proletariat was its leader. Already independent action by the Negro masses in the North is at last awakening organized labor to the fact that it must approach the Negro problem not merely as a trade union, but a social and national problem. This new development helps to clarify and defines the tasks of the party.

The party continues, as it has done in the past, to agitate for equal rights and abolition of Jim Crow in all aspects of industrial and union life. The party views with great satisfaction the remarkable progress made by the CIO in its appreciation of the Negro problem as a union problem. The party fights against the Klan and other Negro-baiting elements in the unions but does not allow the outbreaks against Negroes which have taken place in Detroit, Mobile, and elsewhere to obscure the steady progress in this field.

The party, however, goes beyond mere progressive trade-unionism. It places before the union movement the grave danger that the very existence of a Negro question in the country poses for the union movement and the country as a whole.

The party warns the labor movement that the fascists and pro-fascist elements in their efforts to batter down organized labor, will not fail to use the growing racial tension in the country as the Nazis used anti-semitism in Germany.

The party warns the labor movement that the coming unemployment will create grave dangers for the labor movement, particularly in developing antagonisms between white and Negro labor. The party points out the dangerous situation in the South and the continuous reactionary and anti-labor activity of the Southern Democrats and its basis in the social degradation of the Negroes. The party, therefore, proposes to the labor movement the adoption of its transitional program for a Labor Party as the chief means in the present stage of checking this threat to its very existence. The party boldly poses to the labor movement the necessity of showing the Negroes that labor recognizes its responsibility for solving their problems by radical measure. Labor will thus draw to itself the militant power of the vast majority of oppressed Negroes and will enormously increase its social and political power in the country.

Such sponsoring of the Negro cause will draw the attention of all the other oppressed groups in society to labor's role. It will give enormous confidence and pride to labor itself. It will create a powerful sentiment of good will and respect for the American proletariat among the great masses in Europe, Africa, and Asia. The propaganda of the party in this respect must be bold, comprehensive, and powerful in its insistence on the dangers to society and the continuing shame of the Negro problem, the necessity of proletarian solution, and the gains, direct and indirect, which will follow even the first decisive steps taken by labor.

The party in its daily agitation draws attention of the union movement to the concrete danger represented by the outbreaks which have occurred in recent months and which sooner or later will recur with probably greater violence. The party emphatically urges the union movement to place the responsibility unequivocally upon the enemies of the Negro people. It urges the unions to recognize that the aggressive spirit of the Negro people is the result of their unending oppression. *Organized labor must not discourage, but must stimulate this militancy as one of the surest defenses of democracy not only for Negroes but for organized labor itself and all the oppressed classes.*

The party urges the labor movement to take the lead in organizing this militancy and linking it to the struggle for the reconstruction of society. To white workers complaining of Negro "excesses" the party points out, with restraint yet inflexibly, the great importance of the Negro mass struggle and relegates these complaints to their proper subordinate sphere. Above all, it points out that in conflicts between Negroes and whites in the Negro community, the labor movement must avoid appearing in any light which may be interpreted as a "guardian of the peace," merely anxious to restore the *status quo*. Only by assisting the Negro movement to express its militancy in effective channels and by militantly advocating both an immediate and a general program for the Negroes as a whole, will the labor movement be able to act effectively in times of crisis and yet avoid the multiple dangers of merely acting as a peace-maker. In all Negro manifestations of resistance the organized labor movement must play a leading and active part. The party must unceasingly teach labor that the way to ensure that the resistance of Negroes is directed against capital and its allies is for labor to encourage, organize, and support them to its fullest capacity.

The party will remember that propaganda and agitation of this scope is of special importance for it is being carried out by no other political groups. In the present critical period when many are being more and more impelled to think beyond their immediate interests, the Negro question forms a particularly valuable means of educating the advanced workers in the general principles of socialism and mass revolutionary struggle. The party will point out that because the Negroes have insisted on struggle, and owing to the sympathetic attitude of labor due to the large number of Negroes in its ranks, the Negro struggle in Detroit has developed a logic of its own. This has resulted in a political alliance at the recent elections between organized labor and the Negro community as a whole. Despite the loss of the election, this combination is one of the most significant stages yet reached in the struggle of labor and the Negro masses for emancipation from the ills and injustices of capitalist society. It is along these lines with militant effort on both sides complementing each other that the party must seek, according to its strength, to direct the developing struggle. *Organized labor must learn to turn to its own advantage the increasing radical consciousness and organization which accompanies the integration of the Negro into the social functions of capitalist society.*

The Workers Party and Negro Work Among Negroes

The Negroes Struggle for Democratic Rights and Socialism

The party makes powerful and insistent propaganda to the Negroes that the leadership of organized labor is necessary and indispensable to their successful struggle for democratic rights. Particularly in this time of crisis, it poses to them socialism as the only solution of their problem. It analyzes the economic roots of racial oppression. It emphasizes, above all, the role of competition between members of the working class in destroying white and Negro solidarity. It stresses the national leadership of labor without which the achievement of democratic rights is impossible. It emphasizes the fundamentally class nature of racial oppression and the objective unity of the oppressed in the struggle for socialism.

At the same time the party, with the fullest consciousness of the significance of the mass independent struggles of the Negroes, considers that its main agitational work among Negroes is the stimulation and encouragement of these mass struggles. Basing itself upon one of the most fundamental principles of Marxism, the party recognizes that it is only on the basis of the continual deepening and broadening of their independent mass struggles that the Negro people will ultimately be brought to recognize that organized labor is their only genuine ally in their struggle and that their struggle is part of the struggle for socialism.

The party, in stimulating the independent struggles of the Negro people, teaches Marxism to them in the only terms in which they will learn it, the terms of their own desires and experiences. Thus as the present stage of capitalist development in America, the party seeks wherever possible and feasible to concentrate the attention of the Negro masses upon the responsibility of the government for their oppressed condition. It therefore teaches to the Negroes continuously that the state is the executive committee of the ruling class and on this basis seeks to mobilize them in their own way and according to their own instinctive desires, against the capitalist state and its dominating role in contemporary society.

The party brings Marxism to the Negroes by emphasizing to them that the emancipation of the working class must be the work of the working class itself. It emphasizes to the Negroes that Negro emancipation cannot take place without the vigorous and self-sacrificing struggle of the Negroes themselves. It sharply condemns that distortion of Marxist truth which states or implies that the Negroes by their independent struggles cannot get to first base without the leadership of organized labor.

The party is on the alert to stimulate and encourage every instinctive tendency to independent organization and militant struggle of the Negro masses objectively directed against American capitalism. The history of the Negro people has shown them fertile in the creation and organization of such struggles, and it is on the basis of analysis and criticism of these creative efforts that the party seeks to exercise its special guiding and correcting influence. It is only by this means that it can help direct the efforts of the Negro masses into channels most powerful and fruitful for their own aims and for this very reason most valuable in developing the general struggle for socialism.

The party encourages the masses of the Negro people to seek the assistance of the organized labor movement in the organization of their own defense and in all the stages of their battle for democratic rights. But in its agitation it encourages them to do so for the specific purpose, first of all, of gaining their own democratic demands. *Under no circumstances does it submerge the specific purpose of this alliance in the minds of the Negro people under any general terms of the fight for socialism.* The recognition by the masses of the Negro people that organized labor is their ally in their struggle for their democratic rights can prove a far more powerful step toward socialism than the acceptance by a few Negroes of the theoretic principles of Marxism. It is from the general recognition by the masses of the alliance between the Negro struggle for democratic rights and organized labor that the possibility arises of winning not one or two but dozens of Negro militants for the revolutionary party.

The Negro Proletariat

The role of the Negro proletariat belongs mainly to the general development of the union and organized labor movement as a whole. The party must be on its guard to scrutinize all policies which may deflect the Negro proletariat in the labor movement from considering itself first and foremost as an integral part of the struggle of organized labor for the rights of labor and for socialism. The oppression of the Negroes as a national minority specifically prepares the Negro proletariat in the organized labor movement for a place in the very vanguard of the struggle for socialism.

The Negro proletariat, however, has a special role to play in the struggle of the Negro community for its democratic rights. The party will stimulate the Negro proletariat within the Negro communities to take the lead in the struggle for Negro democratic rights in accordance with the role of labor in modern society. The Negro community and Negro organizations must be stimulated to use the Negro proletariat as its representative to the organized labor movement in its demand for assistance and organization of the struggle for Negro democratic rights. The link in the struggle for Negro democratic rights is between the Negro community as a whole and organized labor and not between the Negro proletariat alone and the white proletariat.

In the present stage the party must conduct, to the extent of its resources, a vigorous and unfailing propaganda and agitation along the above lines. The present situation offers a fertile field for such work among the Negro masses. The experience of the party with its agitation on the Harlem demonstration has already shown how receptive the Negro masses and Negro proletarian elements would be to agitation of this kind.

The party is certain to reap concrete results because there is not at the present time a single labor or radical organization which looks upon the militant Negro demonstration as anything else except at best justifiable because of unfortunate necessities. This means the party will be listened to eagerly by the Negro masses.

The party needs to analyze carefully and draw the lessons of such outbreaks as that in Harlem. Only thus will it be able to offer guidance to the Negroes and to the proletariat, jointly with them to prepare for future outbreaks, and jointly study the revolutionary development of the American masses. Every "minor" crisis in a capitalist state, says Lenin, discloses to us in miniature the elements and germs of the battles which must inevitably take place on a large scale during a big crisis.

The Harlem demonstration was no "minor" strike. It was, as has been shown, an organized demonstration, a Negro nationalist protest, on a stage far higher than Garveyism, involving actively or sympathetically tens of thousands of people. On the day of the demonstration could be seen on one side the masses of the people and on the other, "keeping order," the local municipality (La Guardia), the Social-Democracy (Crosswaithe), the Stalinists (Max Yergan and Hope Stevens), the Negro petty bourgeoisie (Walter White and Lester Granger). Dewey announced that he held in reserve the armed forces of the state. These formed one united group while the masses in the streets booed at them.

The party must resolutely take its place with the protesting masses and expose continuously the unity of those arrayed against them. The party will not adopt merely the attitude of explaining why the masses take such steps. It corrects the exaggerations and mistakes of the masses, but as one of them, taking part in the struggle with them, and seeing to increase and to direct their justified anger into more constructive channels. In the Marxist tradition it subordinates all to the fact that the masses have refused passively to endure injustices and have violently expressed their hatred. The party propagates these ideas and condemns the judicial or explanatory or social-work attitude. It is only on this basis that the party, which is then more certain to get the ear of the masses, can help them to realize their mistakes, and help them to organize greater, more powerful, and more effective demonstrations which can in turn become nation-wide militant movements.

The Party and the Negro Nationalist Movements

The party wages a merciless war against the Negro nationalist movements such as the Garveyites, the pro-Japanese organization, etc. It demonstrates their fantastic and reactionary proposals for Negro emancipation. It explains in detail the utter impossibility of their realization and, furthermore, takes the trouble to explain that even if these were realized, it would not in any way benefit the great masses of the Negro people. The party seizes this opportunity to analyze and denounce the imperialism of the Japanese and the oppression of the Japanese masses. Thus in terms of the Negro's own life and interests it builds a sentiment of solidarity of the oppressed on an international scale.

At the same time, however, the party must study these movements carefully, to differentiate between the Negro nationalist leaders and their sincere but misguided followers. It explains to the masses that the desire for the success of Japan is in reality a desire for the destruction of the apparently unbreakable power of their own oppressor, American imperialism, and the humbling of its pride. The impending defeat of Japan will strike a heavy blow at any hopes of assistance, direct or indirect, to the "colored peoples" from a Japanese victory. The national movements, however, even before the defeat of Japan, used Garveyism and pro-Japanese sentiment merely as an ideological basis for a policy directed towards strengthening Negro nationalism in the United States. The movements which seek "to drive the Jew out of Harlem or the South Side" have a valid class base. They are the reactions of the resentful Negro seeking economic relief and some salve for his humiliated racial pride. That these sentiments can be exploited by fanatical idiots, Negro anti-Semites, or self-seeking Negro business men, does not alter their fundamentally progressive basis. This progressiveness is in no way to be confused with the dissatisfaction of the demoralized white petty-bourgeoisie which seeks refuge in fascism. American reaction can and probably will finance or encourage some of these movements (Bilbo and Back to Africa) in order to feed ill will. But the Negroes are overwhelmingly proletarian, semi-proletarian, and peasant in their class composition. Such is the whole course of American history that any nation-wide Fascist movement (however disguised) will be compelled to attack the Negro struggle for equality. But the struggle for equality is the main driving force of the Negro mass movement.

The party, therefore, while boldly attacking the nationalist movement, does not in any way treat these movements in the same category as it would a fascist movement. It attacks them upon the basis of a program for Negro struggle as outlined above. It is the absence of a comprehensive program and action for Negro rights and Negro struggle advanced by organized labor; it is the sectarian presentation of the doctrine of the Negro struggle as class struggle which gives strength to the nationalists. Such is the obvious bankruptcy of the nationalists' magic-carpet programs for salvation in all parts of the world that their chief strength, in Harlem for instance, is due not to their programs but to their active role in protests and demonstrations designed to improve the conditions of the Negroes here in America.

The Party and the Negro Petty Bourgeoisie

An economic examination of the American scene will demonstrate how slight is the economic basis of the Negro petty bourgeoisie. The Negro petty bourgeoisie is for the most part a woefully disproportionate group of intelligentsia, well-paid domestics, stage performers, etc. Bourgeois society has rigidly excluded them not only from social contact with the whites but also from those positions and opportunities of sharing in the surplus value, and gaining distinction, which binds so many of the white petty bourgeois functionaries to bourgeois society. They can do harm as in the March on Washington Committee, but their impotence to restrain the masses of the Negroes when these are anxious to move has been demonstrated during the past period. Such influence as, for instance, the Indian nationalist bourgeoisie has exercised over the Indian masses, the Negro petty bourgeoisie can never exercise over the Negroes. The party observes that the instinct for direct action of the Negro masses ignored the NAACP or the Urban League, as circumstances dictated. But the party is on the alert to enter those newer organizations which the Negroes are forming today in such profusion, if even sometimes for only very limited purposes.

The party keeps up an unceasing attack on the Negro petty-bourgeois leaders, but is careful to do so, not on general grounds, but because they do not carry on a militant struggle for democratic rights and betray the struggle at every opportunity. In this respect the party attacks the petty-bourgeois leaders of the Negroes in a manner approximating its attacks on the labor leadership of the social democracy.

The Negroes and the Labor Party

The party must carry on a militant agitation among the Negroes on behalf of an independent Labor Party. It is a sign of their special role in American society and the maturing social consciousness of the Negro people that as a body they have made within the last few years a rapid change in their attitude toward organized labor. Should organized labor put forward a militant program for an independent Labor Party the past history of Negroes and present indications show that the movement of the Negroes in its favor will be strong and perhaps overwhelming. The Negroes in all probability will play a role in the left wing of the organization. But here also the Negroes' situation as specially oppressed minority, though not necessarily obtruded, must be taken into consideration. An independent Labor Party in the United States as in many European countries will probably consist of a federation of various groups, with the union movement providing the base, the driving force, and the leadership.

The independent labor party will not tolerate any distinction of color within its ranks. Local non-union organizations of all types will seek affiliation. Negroes should be encouraged to join such local affiliations. *But the party must carry on a vigorous agitation among militant Negro organizations struggling for Negro democratic rights not only to join the agitation for an independent labor party but also to take an active part in its formation.*

At the present stage of capitalist crisis in the U.S. this particular work by the party offers exceptional means of forming a bridge between the independent struggle of the Negro masses and the general problem of the reconstruction of society.

The Negro organizations should be encouraged themselves to formulate demands for their own democratic rights. The party must insist that neither the Democratic nor the Republican Party is the type of organization which will be able to give the Negroes an opportunity to struggle for these rights within a broader framework. At the same time, even to the most nationalistic of the Negro organizations, the party should pose the question of themselves forming a program not only for Negro democratic rights but for the country as a whole. They must look, not to European imperialism in Africa nor to Japanese imperialism, but to potential allies in this country and make their own contribution to the elaboration of that type of social order in which the Negroes will at last find equality. This must be presented to the Negro organizations as an imperative duty for Negro organizations to perform. It is by this means that the Negroes, on the basis of their own nationalistic preoccupations, are brought to consider their own problems in relation to the fundamental problem of the whole social order. The party will seize this opportunity to present its own transitional program to Negroes, for them to consider in the light of their intense desire for some solution, not only immediate but general, to the degradation from which they have suffered to so many centuries.

Such is the proletarian composition of the Negro people, so hostile are they to existing social order *because of the special degradation to which it subjects them,* that the political organization which knows how to utilize their preoccupation with their democratic right can find ample ways and means for carrying on that socialistic propaganda which must always be the climax of revolutionary effort, particularly in this period. Starting from and never ignoring the basis of the independent struggles for democratic rights, the party will find in the increasing contradictions in the social order the possibility of uniting in ever higher stages of development of the objective movement of the American proletariat toward leadership of the nation and the movement of the masses of Negro people toward the American proletariat.

Negro Chauvinism

The history of the Negro in the U.S. is a history of his increasing race
consciousness, a constantly increasing desire to vindicate his past and the
achievements and qualifications of the Negro race as a race. This is an
inevitable result of his position in American society, of the development
of this society itself, and is not only a powerful but a familiar concomitant
everywhere of the struggles of nationally oppressed groups. It does not grow
less with the social development of the oppressed and the oppressing groups.
*On the contrary, it increases in direct ratio with the development of capitalism and
the possibilities of liberation.* This was recognized by the Socialist Workers
Party in its 1939 convention when it adopted a resolution which stated
in part:

> " . . . the awakening political consciousness of the Negro not unnaturally
> takes the form of a desire for independent action uncontrolled by whites.
> The Negroes have long felt and more than ever feel today the urge to
> create their own organizations under their own leaders and thus assert,
> not only in theory but in action, their claim to complete equality with
> other American citizens. Such a desire is legitimate and even when it
> takes the form of a rather aggressive chauvinism is to be welcomed. Black
> chauvinism in America today is merely the natural excess of the desire
> for equality while white American chauvinism, the expression of racial
> domination, is essentially reactionary."

So clear is this development that today even the bourgeoisie is recognizing it. In *An American Dilemma* by Gunnar Myrdal, despite its petty-
bourgeois humanitarian attitude, there has at last appeared a serious,
comprehensive, and, in many respects, authoritative study of the Negro
question. One of its final conclusions is that: "Negroes are beginning to
form a self-conscious 'nation within a nation,' defining ever more clearly
their fundamental grievances against white America." Such a movement
with such deep historical roots must inevitably bring exaggerations, excesses
and ideological trends for which the only possible name is chauvinism. This
trend undoubtedly has dangers. Marxism both in theory and in practice
has demonstrated that the only way to overcome them is to recognize its
fundamentally progressive tendency and to distinguish sharply between the
chauvinism of the oppressed and the chauvinism of the oppressor. The duty
of the party is not only to lead the legitimate aspirations of the Negro masses
but also to educate organized labor as a whole as to the legitimacy of the
feelings of the great masses of the Negro people and the great contributions

which this can become to the struggle for socialism. Despite all apparent difficulties, a bold and confident policy on the part of our party has every possibility of success. The reason for this is simple. *Whereas in Europe the national movements have usually aimed as a separation from the oppressing power, in the U.S. the race consciousness and chauvinism of the Negro represents fundamentally a consolidation of his forces for the purposes of integration into American society.*

The Negro Question as an International Question

The Negro question, i.e., the question of slavery, in the U.S. during the nineteenth century excited amazing interest and action among the international proletariat. The emancipation of the Negro slaves and the Civil War are indissolubly connected with the foundation of the First International. The Third International recognized this aspect of the Negro question when in its Resolution on the Negro Question at the Fourth Congress it not only reiterated the support of the Comintern for revolutionary Negro struggles but devoted a special section to the importance of the role which Negroes in the U.S. could play in the emancipation of Negroes all over the world and particularly in Africa. Today the process of historical development and capitalist disintegration have carried the Negro question in the U.S. a stage further in its international relations. Not only among the British masses does the Negro question occupy a foremost place as a test of American democracy but all over the world and particularly in the Oriental countries the situation and struggle of the Negro people in the United States has become one of the criteria by which oppressed nationalities test the possibilities of their own emancipation.

Among the American Negroes themselves the role and fate of India, of China, and of Burma in their struggle for emancipation is recognized as being connected with their own struggles. The Negro press has consistently devoted many pages to the struggles of the Oriental peoples, and the *Pittsburgh Courier* has two regular weekly columns, one by an Indian and one by a Chinese. Negro organizations, in their common manifesto to both the Republican and Democratic conventions of 1944, made "the equality of China" with all the Allied nations, one of their fundamental demands. It is the function of the Fourth International to develop and to clarify this instinctive striving of the people towards internationalism. With the utmost seriousness the party must recognize and expound the historic roots of this development and direct it toward the education and organization of the international proletariat and its present allies in the struggles for world socialism.

Program of Action

I. The first requisite is the systematic education of the party in the Negro question. In the period which we are entering, the period of world upheaval and social crises in America, the party members must above all on this difficult and complicated question have a clear theoretical orientation. In *The New International* and in internal bulletins there must be a series of informed studies and discussions on the Marxist interpretation of the development of the Negro in the history of the United States. Such studies do not exist in the U.S. at all except for some beginning by the Stalinists. It is impossible for the party to make any serious and continued progress in Negro work without some such preparation. For the time being we merely outline a few of the topics which can be immediately considered:

(a) The Negroes in the Civil War. The Civil War is as much the theoretical axis of American analysis as the French Revolution is for modern Europe. And central to the Civil War is slavery, i.e. the Negro question.

(b) The Negroes in the organized labor movement, their historical development in this movement, and the interrelation of the Negro community and these struggles.

(c) Negro organizations in the recent past and in the present, particularly the Garvey movement as the greatest Negro mass movement which U.S. history can show.

(d) The Negro in Southern agriculture.

(e) Negro social development and political struggles in Africa and the West Indies.

(f) The concrete experiences of the WP in Negro work.

These studies, for the most part, are, first of all, matters of fact, but are also matters of interpretation. It is practically a virgin field not only for the party but for all Marxists in the U.S. They are therefore and for a long time must be mainly matters of discussion. It is through attention to these questions that the party will educate its members and enable them to represent Marxism among the Negroes and within the ranks of organized labor. It is by this means also that the party will be able to influence and to direct the always alert interest of a nationally oppressed people to whatever deals with its national oppression, however unpopular or distasteful the general ideas of a revolutionary group might otherwise be. As a first prerequisite it is necessary to publish the notes and observations of Trotsky on the Negro question.

2. The National Committee must, in accordance with the practice and tradition of the Bolshevik movement, organize a special Negro department to deal with the general work among Negroes. This work must in no way be subordinated to the work among Negroes in the organized labor movement, which is more specifically the work of the trade union department. The work of both departments must be coordinated.

The Negro department should be responsible for a special column in the newspaper on the Negro question and should invite the participation of non-party sympathizers in its theoretical work.

FIVE

Historical Sketches

I. African Civilization

To know where the Negro is going one must know where the Negro comes from. Capitalist history and capitalist science, taken as a whole, are designed to serve the needs of capitalist profit. Their studies of the Negro and his history have aimed at justifying his exploitation and degradation. They have excused the slave trade and slavery and the present position of Negroes as outcasts in capitalist society, on the ground that the Negro in Africa had shown himself incapable of developing civilization, that he lived a savage and barbarous life, and that such elements of culture as Africa showed in the past and shows today were directly due to the influence of Arabs and Europeans. All of this, from beginning to end, is lies.

First of all, the capitalist scientist's attempts to isolate the "pure" Negro from other African peoples is admitted today to be pure rubbish. Though there are broad differentiations, the Negroes in Africa are inextricably mixed. There are people of Hamitic stock who derive either from the Near East or the outermost peninsula of Africa (today British and Italian Somaliland). There are the short-statured Bushmen in the South and the supposedly "pure" Negro is found on the West Coast alone. It is as if a scientist said that the "pure" European was found only on the coast of Portugal. The truth is that even the Egyptians had a strong Negroid strain. There were Negro dynasties in Egypt. Queen Nefertiti, one of the great conquerors and rulers of Egyptian history, was reputedly a Negress. Among the modern Ethiopian ruling class can be seen types, ranging from the purely Semitic through the Mulatto to types indistinguishable from the Negro.

The chief object of these scientists is of course to deprive the Negro of any share in the famous civilizations of Egypt and Ethiopia. Today, ingenious Negroes call the Egyptians "black men" and by this means place all Egyptian civilization to the credit of the Negro. Racial theories of this type, whether from white capitalist centers of learning or fanatical Negro nationalists, are neither history nor science, but political propaganda. This much is clear and for the time being sufficient: the Egyptian civilization began where it did and flourished because of favorable climactic and geographical conditions, and the Negroes had a great deal to do with it.

The attempt to deduce from history that Negroes are subhuman continually breaks down. The Bushmen are among the most primitive of peoples. Yet their drawings have been universally hailed as some of the most marvelous examples of artistic skill. And since when have monkeys been given to producing great artists? In South Africa the ruins of Zimbabwe are evidence of a great ancient civilization. Whose? Nobody knows, but numerous professors are racking their brains to prove that, whoever created it, it wasn't Negroes. Much good may it do them. They will not stop the world revolution that way.

But the greatest stumbling block in the way of the anti-Negro historians are the empires of Ghana, Songhay, Mos, and others, which flourished in the basin of the Niger. People who sneer at the Marxist phrase "bourgeois ideology" simply have no conception of the dishonesty, corruption, and scope of capitalist lies and propaganda.

For nearly a thousand years (300–1300), between the River Senegal and the Niger flourished the Ghana empire. We do not know how it was founded. Some people say that a Hamitic people from East Africa migrated there. Others say that they came from Syria. What we do know is that this empire at its zenith embraced many millions of people. It produced wool, cotton, silk, velvet; it traded in copper and gold. Many houses in the chief towns were built of stone. At one time its army consisted of 200,000 soldiers. Its schools, its lawyers, its scholars were famous all over the Mediterranean area. And this empire for nearly a thousand years was an empire of black men, of Negroes.

Another famous empire was that of Songhay (600–1500) with its dynasty of Askias. Askia Mohammed I (1493–1528) was not only a great ruler. He surrounded himself with scholars. Timbuktu and Gao were the centers of trade and learning.

The latest edition of the *Encyclopedia Britannica* says of these kingdoms, "Long before the rise of Islam, the peoples of this Northern part of West Africa, consisting largely, as has been seen, of open plains watered by large and navigable rivers, had developed well-organized states, of which the oldest known, Ghana (or Ghanata) is thought to have been founded in the third century A.D. Later arose the empire of Melle and the more famous and more powerful Songhoi (Songhoy) empire. . . . Marking the importance, commercial and political, of these states, large cities were founded." The ideas that Islamic influences founded these states is now exploded, and this is admitted by the *Britannica* writer. He follows, however, the theory of "pure" and "impure" Negroes. The Negroes on the coast were "pure." But even these, he notes, founded civilizations: " . . . the Yoruba, the Ashanti, the Dahomi, and the Beni created powerful and well organized kingdoms."

The Beni, better know as the Benin, are famous today for their bronze sculpture, of artistic merit and technical skill unsurpassed by any people of ancient or modern times. When after many centuries they were "discovered" in 1891, the impudent imperialists at once attributed these bronzes to "Portuguese" influence. That theory has now joined the other in the waste-paper basket.

West Africa was the high-water mark. But all over Africa, organized civilizations flourished. The first Portuguese to visit East Africa some five hundred years ago did not remark any noticeable differences between the Africans and themselves; while less than fifty years ago, Emil Torday, the Belgian explorer, discovered in Central Africa the Bushongo people. A wise king, as far back as the seventeenth century, had prohibited all contact with Europeans, and, away in his interior, the tribe had survived. Torday found a free and happy people, living in villages well laid out, the huts beautifully decorated, their sculpture, textiles, and household objects of a rare beauty. Political organization was a perfect democracy. The king had all the honors, the council all the power. Representatives, two of them always women, were both regional and vocational. Today they are degraded savages. Torday states that before the coming of the Europeans such civilizations, perfectly adapted to their environment, were widespread over Africa. The picture of warring tribes and savage cannibals is all lies.

As late as 1906, Frobenius traveling in the Belgian Congo, could still see the following: "And on all this flourishing material, civilization then was abloom; here the bloom on ripe fruit both tender and lustrous; the gestures, manners, and customs of a whole people, from the youngest to the oldest, alike in the families of the princes and the well-to-do, of the slaves, so naturally dignified and refined in the smallest detail. I know no northern race who can bear comparison with such a uniform level of education as is found among the natives."

It was the slave trade that destroyed Africa, the depredations of Arabs and European imperialists. They ravaged the continent for three centuries. What the travellers of the nineteenth century discovered was the wreck and ruin of what had existed four centuries before, and even then enough remained to disprove the ideas of the subhuman Negro. Africa is a vast continent and many millions of people in varying degrees of civilization have lived there over the centuries. There was much ignorance, barbarism, and superstition, but the history and achievements of Negroes in art, literature, politics, empire-building, until Arab and European imperialism fell upon them in the twelfth and thirteenth centuries, is an incontrovertible refutation of the mountains of lies and slander built up by capitalist apologists in defense of capitalist barbarism. Africans worked in iron countless generations ago and many historians claim that it was they who introduced metal work to Europe and Asia.

Capitalism developing in Europe precipitated the discovery of America and sent its navigators and explorers to Africa. In the sixteenth century began the use of Negro slaves in the plantations of America. British capitalism drew one of the most powerful sources of wealth from the slave trade. The greatness of Liverpool, the second city of Great Britain, was founded on the trade. The wealth of the French bourgeoisie was based upon the slave trade. The rise of modern Europe is inexplicable without a knowledge of the economic ramifications of the slave trade.

II. Emancipation from Slavery and the Destruction of Feudalism

First of all, what is feudalism? That is not easy to answer in a sentence. It is a form of society based on landed property and simple methods of cultivation.

They have a landowning class which rules; at the other end of the social scale you have the serfs, who get a part of their produce to feed themselves and contribute their surplus to the landowning aristocracy. Side by side with the landowning aristocracy is the clergy. The main characteristic of social life in feudal society is the fact that the aristocracy and clergy have great privileges, and the serfs and others have very few or none. This is not a question of custom, but a question of law. (In capitalist society, in theory, all men are equal before the law.)

Feudal economy in Europe did not in any way have contact with Africa. It was essentially a subsistence economy; that is to say, it produced what it needed to feed and clothe itself. About the thirteenth and fourteenth centuries, however, there grew up in Europe a new class, the merchants. These were the first real capitalists.

Soon their business began to be of great importance in the state. With increasing wealth, they gradually changed the economies of certain countries from producing chiefly food and the simple things that the community needed, to the manufacture of goods on a large scale. This particular class was concerned as much with production for trade in other parts of the country and abroad as for use at home. It was this drive for trade, for raw materials, for markets, and for profit, that created the necessity for expansion, and in the fifteenth century finally sent expeditions to America and to Africa. Thus it was the development of capitalism in Europe that brought the millions of Africans into contact with Western civilization.

Capitalism demands above all else landless laborers. In Europe the capitalist class created a class of landless laborers by driving them off the land whenever possible, for if the serf or the peasant had land on which to work or earn his keep for himself, naturally he would not hire himself out to any capitalist for long hours and small pay.

When the capitalists discovered America, they tried to use the Indian as landless laborers. But the Indians died. There was so much land that it was impossible to get landless laborers from among the early colonists. Because of this, the capitalists in Europe and their agents in the colonies brought millions of Negroes as slaves to America and thereby provided the colonies with the necessary labor. By this means capitalism enormously expanded its capacity for making profit.

By means of these vast profits that they made at home and abroad, the capitalists in Britain and France, for example not only built up tremendous trade and business, but with the profits accumulated, they began to organize factories and extend the application of science to industry. The standard of civilization rose, and the power and profits of the capitalists increased also. But the governments of France and Britain still continued to be under the domination of the old feudal nobility. When came much trouble.

Trade and factories were more important than land. Yet the rulers of the countries were princes, dukes, lords, bishops, and archbishops. That was all very well when they had the economic power, but now it had passed from them. Not only were they proud and arrogant, but they tried to keep the laws and the government suitable to land ownership when, owing to the shift in the economic basis of the country, the laws and the government should have been organized to help trade and industry. It was no use pointing out to them that they should give way. It took revolutions to do it.

In Britain there were two revolutions. One took place in the seventeenth century and lasted off and on for nearly sixty years. In France, revolution began in 1789, and by the time it was over the power of the aristocracy and the clergy was wiped away completely.

What part did the Negroes play in all this?

The capitalists who first profited by slavery were commercial capitalists and the planters in the colonies. These planters were partly capitalist in that they traded their produce far and wide, and partly feudal in that they kept their slaves in a state of subjection comparable to the old serfdom and built up a type of feudal society. But as capitalism developed, these commercial traders and the plantation owners collaborated closely with the aristocracy, and many of them became aristocrats themselves. By the time the industrial capitalists were busy developing their factories, the aristocrats, the planters, and the commercial capitalists formed, roughly speaking, one reactionary group.

Now one of the things that the industrial capitalists wanted to do was to finish with slavery. It was too expensive. Slave production was backward compared with modern methods and more highly developed capitalist production in agriculture. So that you had on one side the industrial capitalists determined to destroy the slave power of the aristocrats, the commercial capitalists, and the planters. It was in this political struggle that Negroes got their chance to fight for their freedom. They played a small part in the English political struggle, a larger part in the French struggle, and a decisive part in the American struggle. This was not accidental. A few figures will show us why.

In 1789 British colonial trade was five million pounds out of an export trade of 27 million. Britain had lost America in 1783 and had few slaves in the West Indies. We can therefore see that slavery was playing a very minor part in British economy. The British Negroes on the whole played little part in the destruction of British feudalism.

In France in 1789 the export trade was 17 million pounds. The colonial trade was 11 million pounds—two thirds of it. The question of abolition was therefore of tremendous importance. It took a prominent part in the revolution. The Negroes fought magnificently and, being thousands of miles away, gained their independence. This is how Haiti came into being.

In America in 1861 this combination of the commercial bourgeoisie and the plantation owners was not a minor part of American economy. It was a major part. The combination was not a colony thousands of miles away. It occupied hundreds of thousands of square miles inside the country. To defeat this combination took the greatest Civil War in history, and the Negro's share was far greater than it had been in France.

This is the way we must look at history. People who only see black men in general being oppressed by white men in general, and are unable to trace the historical dialectic, do not understand anything and therefore cannot lead. That is the great value of being a genuine Marxist, an adherent of the Fourth International. You can study history and understand where we are today and why and where we are going tomorrow.

III. The Bourgeois Revolutions and Imperialism

Let us for a moment review our analysis of the Negro in his contact with Western civilization. . . . We established that the Negroes in Africa had built high if simple civilizations up to the fourteenth century. It was necessary to emphasize this, to destroy the imperialist-fostered conception of Africa as a land of eternal savagery and barbarism from which it has to some degree been raised by the gentle hand of the European invaders.

European contact with Africa began with the rise of European imperialism. A new continent, America, was discovered and Africa, which had always lain within easy reach of European ships, was penetrated. Commercial capitalism developed the mercantile system, which needed labor in the American tropical plantation. When the Indians proved unsatisfactory, slaves were brought from Africa. On the basis of the wealth created by the slave trade and the colonial trade directly dependent upon it, the commercial capitalists of Europe and America built up from their ranks a new section of the capitalist class, the industrial capitalists. These, whose chief function was the application of large-scale organization and science to industry, came inevitably into conflict with the planters: slave labor was too expensive, too backward for the new methods. This economic conflict was the basis for political conflict. The commercial bourgeoisie and the feudal aristocracy still had the political power their former economic predominance had given them, and for the new rising class of industrial bourgeoisie, to wrest it from them meant a struggle.

This was a progressive struggle. It took place in great revolutions in France and in America, and in Britain it took not only the threat but the actual beginning of a revolution to break the power of the feudal aristocrats. In all these the Negro played a tremendous part. In America he was given the opportunity of doing this because his emancipation was in the interest of the Northern industrialist bourgeoisie. All these great movements of politics thrust the color question into subordination and unimportance. It is economics and politics, not color, that are decisive in history.

To see what happened after the industrialist bourgeoisie took power, it would be best to follow the course of one country, say Great Britain. The industrialists seized power in 1832. They struck a terrific blow at the landed aristocracy in 1847 by abolishing the "corn laws." Through these laws the feudal aristocrats had artificially maintained the price of grain by restricting foreign competition with the produce of their fields. Rising with the industrial bourgeoisie was a new class—the industrial working class, the proletariat. And by 1848 the Chartist Movement of the workers was feeling its way towards revolution.

But in this year began a great era of prosperity. So prosperous was the industrial bourgeoisie, thanks to the home market its victory had given it, that it treated the idea of colonies in Africa with scorn. Disraeli wrote in 1866 that the British had all that they wanted in Asia. For, he continued, "what is the use of these colonial deadweights, the West Indian and West Africa colonies? . . . Leave the Canadians to govern themselves; recall the African squadrons; give up the settlements on the southeast coast of Africa and we shall make a saving which will at the same time enable us to build ships and have a good budget." In the year he wrote, only one-tenth or less of Africa was in the hands of European imperialists. They had devastated the continent, but now they wanted the slaves no longer. For a while it almost seemed that Africa would be left in peace.

But capitalist production lead inevitable to the concentration of wealth in the hands of a few and the corresponding increasing poverty of the masses. The workers cannot buy what they produce. The capitalists must find abroad new markets, sources of new materials, and places to invest their capital.

In 1885 Jules Ferry, the French statesman, used the famous words:

> Colonies for rich countries are one of the most lucrative methods of utilizing capital. . . . I say that France, which is glutted with capital, has a reason for looking on this side of the colonial question. . . . European consumption is saturated: it is necessary to raise new masses of consumer in other parts of the globe, else we shall put modern society into bankruptcy and prepare for social liquidation with the dawn of the twentieth century. . . .

Cecil Rhodes once told a friend, "If you want to free civilization, become an imperialist." With the glut in the home market, colonies were no longer "deadweight." While in 1880 only one-tenth of Africa was in the hands of European imperialists; by 1900 less than one-tenth of the land remained in the hands of the African people. That saturation of European consumption to which Ferry referred and the part that Africa played can be shown by the following simple calculation. Great Britain has invested abroad roughly twenty billion dollars. The total investment in Africa from all sources is roughly six billion dollars, and of this almost five billion is in British territory. That is to say, almost one-fourth of British foreign investment is to be found in Africa.

But this process of "saturation" that forced the imperialists to expand to the colonies has now itself spread to the colonies. The increasing accumulation of great wealth in the hands of the few and the increasing poverty of the masses is now not only a European but world phenomenon. Imperialism, the highest stage of capitalism, is bankrupt. The war of 1914–1918, the worldwide crisis since 1929, the new world war of 1939—these are items from the ledger of imperialism. Only the overthrowing of the bankrupt class by a new class, only the triumphant proletarian revolution, can balance the budget of civilization.

And in the same way as the Negro played an important role in the revolution of the industrialists in unseating the feudal aristocracy, so tomorrow the Negroes will play a decisive role in the struggle between finance-capital and the working class. Against his declared intentions, Lincoln was forced to free the slaves. Revolutionary France had to recognize the revolution of the Santo Domingo blacks. In the stress of economic and political conflict, color was forgotten and the rising class took help wherever it could get it. The Negroes in Africa and America, wherever they are the most oppressed of people, are going to strike even more deadly blows for freedom, against the capitalist system of exploitation, in alliance with the white workers of the world.

NEGROES IN THE CIVIL WAR: THEIR ROLE IN THE SECOND AMERICAN REVOLUTION (1943)

An indisputable contribution to the understanding of the role of the Negro in American history is a study of the period between 1830 and 1865. In this article we treat the subject up to 1860.

The basic economic and social antagonisms of the period embraced the whole life of the country and were fairly clear then, far less so today. The system of chattel slavery needed territorial expansion because of the soil exhaustion caused by the crude method of slave production. But as the North developed industrially and in population, the South found it ever more difficult to maintain its political domination. Finally the struggle centered, economically, around who would control the newly-opened territories, and, politically, around the regional domination of Congress.

The regime in the South was 1830 a dreadful tyranny, in startling contrast to the vigorous political democracy in the North. The need to suppress the slaves, who rebelled continuously, necessitated a regime of naked violence. The need to suppress the hostility to slavery of the free laborers and independent farmers led to the gradual abrogation of all popular democracy in the Southern states.

Previously in 1830 there had been anti-slavery societies in the South itself, but by 1830 cotton was king and, instead of arguing for and against slavery, the Southern oligarchy gradually developed a theory of Negro slavery as a heaven-ordained dispensation. Of necessity they sought to impose it upon the whole country. Such a propaganda can be opposed only actively. Not to oppose it is to succumb to it.

The impending revolution is to be led by the Northern bourgeoisie. But that is the last thing that it wants to do. In 1776 the revolutionary struggle was between the rising American bourgeoisie and a foreign enemy. The bourgeoisie needs little prodding to undertake its task. By 1830 the conflict was between two sections of the ruling class based on different economies but tied together by powerful economic links. Therefore, one outstanding feature of the new conflict is the determination of the Northern bourgeois to make every concession and every sacrifice to prevent the precipitation of the break. They will not lead. *They will have to be forced to lead.* The first standard-bearers of the struggle are the petty-bourgeois democracy, organized in the Abolition movement, stimulated and sustained by the independent mass action of the Negro people.

The Petty Bourgeoisie and the Negroes

The petty bourgeoisie, having the rights of universal suffrage, had entered upon a period of agitation which has been well summarized in the title of a modern volume: *The Rise of the Common Man.* Lacking the economic demands of an organized proletariat, this agitation found vent in ever-increasing waves of humanitarianism and enthusiasm for social progress. Women's rights, temperance reform, public education, abolition of privilege, universal peace, the brotherhood of man—middle class intellectual America was in ferment. And to this pulsating movement the rebellious Negroes brought the struggle for the abolition of slavery. The agreement among historians is general that all these diverse trends were finally dominated by the Abolition movement.

The Negro struggle for Abolition follows a pattern not dissimilar to the movement for emancipation before 1776. There are, first of all, the same continuous revolts among the masses of the slaves themselves which marked the pre-1776 period. In the decade 1820–30 devoted white men begin the publication of periodicals which preach Abolition on principled grounds. The chief of these was Benjamin Lundy. No sooner does Lundy give the signal than the free Negroes take it up and become the driving force of the movement.

Garrison, directly inspired by Lundy, began early, in 1831. But before that, Negro Abolitionists, not only in speeches and meetings, but in books, periodicals, and pamphlets, posed the question squarely before the crusading petty bourgeois democracy. *Freedom's Journal* was published in New York City by two Negroes as early as 1827. David Walker's *Appeal*, published in 1829, created a sensation. It was a direct call for revolution. Free Negroes organized conventions and mass meetings. And before the movement was taken over by such figures as Wendell Phillips and other distinguished men of the time, the free Negroes remained the great supporters of the *Liberator*. In 1831, out of 450 subscribers, fully 400 were Negroes. In 1834, of 2300 subscribers, nearly 2000 were Negroes.

After the free Negroes came the masses. When Garrison published the *Liberator* in 1831, the new Abolition movement, as contrasted with the old anti-slavery societies, amount[ed] to little. Within less than a year its fame was nation-wide. What caused this was the rebellion of Nat Turner in 1831. It is useless to speculate whether Walker's *Appeal* or the *Liberator* directly inspired Turner. What is decisive is the effect on the Abolition movement of this, the greatest Negro revolt in the history of the United States.

The Turner revolt not only lifted Garrison's paper and stimulated the organization of his movement. The South responded with such terror that the Negroes, discouraged by the failures of the revolts between 1800 and 1831, began to take another road to freedom. Slowly but steadily grew that flight out of the South which lasted for thirty years and injected the struggle against slavery into the North itself. As early as 1827 the escaping Negroes had already achieved some rudimentary form of organization. It was during the eventful year of 1831 that the Underground Railroad took more definite shape. In time thousands of whites and Negroes risked life, liberty, and often wealth to assist the rebel slaves.

The great body of escaping slaves, of course, had no political aims in mind. For years rebellious slaves had formed bands of maroons, living a free life in inaccessible spots. Thousands had joined the Indians. Now they sought freedom in civilization and they set forth on that heroic journey of many hundreds of miles, forced to travel mainly by night, through forest and across rivers, often with nothing to guide them but the North Star and the fact that moss grows only on the north side of trees.

The industrial bourgeoisie in America wanted none of this Abolition. It organized mobs who were not unwilling to break up meetings and to lynch agitators. Many ordinary citizens were hostile to Negroes because of competition in industry and the traditional racial prejudice. At one period in the early 1840s, the Abolition movement slumped and Negro historians assert that it was the escaping slaves who kept the problem alive and revived the movement. But we do not need the deductions of modern historians. What the escaping slaves meant to the movement leaps to the eye of the Marxian investigator from every contemporary page.

By degrees the leadership of the movement passed into the hands of and was supported by some of the most gifted white poets, writers, and publicists of their time. The free Negroes in collaboration with the Abolitionist movement, sometimes by themselves, carried on a powerful agitation. But a very special role was played by the ablest and most energetic of the escaping slaves themselves. These men could write and speak from first-hand experience. They were a dramatic witness of the falseness and iniquity of the whole thesis upon which the Southern cause was built. Greatest of them all and one of the greatest men of his time was Frederick Douglass, a figure today strangely neglected. In profundity and brilliance, Douglass, the orator, was not the equal of Wendell Phillips. As a political agitator, he did not attain the fire and scope of Garrison nor the latter's dynamic power in organization. But he was their equal in courage, devotion, and tenacity of purpose, and in sheer political skill and sagacity he was definitely their superior. He broke with them early, evolving his own policy of maintenance of the Union as opposed to their policy of disunion. He advocated the use of all means, including the political, to attain Abolition. It was only after many years that the Garrisonians followed his example. Greatest of the activists was another escaped slave, Harriet Tubman. Very close to these ex-slaves was John Brown. These three were the nearest to what we would call today the revolutionary propagandists and agitators.

They drove the South to infuriation. Toward the middle of the century the Abolitionists and the escaping slaves had created a situation that made compromise impossible.

The Anti-Fugitive Slave Law

In 1848 there occurred an extraordinary incident, a harbinger of the great international movement which was to play so great a part in the Civil War itself. When the news of the 1848 revolution in France reached Washington, the capital, from the White House to the crowds in the streets, broke out into illuminations and uproarious celebration. Three nights afterward, 78 slaves, taking this enthusiasm for liberty literally, boarded a ship that was waiting for them and tried to escape down the Potomac. They were recaptured and were led back to jail, with a crowd of several thousands waiting in the streets to see them, and members of Congress in the House almost coming to blows in the excitement. The patience of the South and of the Northern bourgeoisie was becoming exhausted. Two years later, the ruling classes, South and North, tried one more compromise.

One of the elements of this compromise was a strong Anti-Fugitive Slave Law. The Southerners were determined to stop this continual drain upon their property and the continuous excitation of the North by fugitive slaves.

It was the impossibility of enforcing the Anti-Fugitive Slave Law which wrecked the scheme. Not only did the slaves continue to leave. Many insurrectionary tremors shook the Southern structure in 1850 and again in 1854. The South now feared a genuine slave insurrection. They had either to secede or force their political demands upon the federal government.

The Northern bourgeoisie was willing to discipline the petty bourgeois democracy. But before long, in addition to their humanitarian drive, the petty bourgeois democrats began to understand that not only the liberty of the slaves but their own precious democratic liberties were at stake. To break the desire of the slaves to escape, and to stifle the nation-wide agitation, the South tried to impose restrictions upon public meetings in the North and upon the use of the mails. They demanded the right to use the civil authorities of the North to capture escaping slaves. Under their pressure, Congress even reached so far as to side-track the right of petition. The Declaration of Independence, when presented as a petition in favor of Abolition, was laid upon the table. Negroes who had lived peaceably in the North for years were now threatened, and thousands fled to Canada. Douglass and Harriet Tubman, people of nation-wide fame (Douglass was an international figure) were in danger. There was no settling this question at all. The petty bourgeois democrats defied the South. The escaping slaves continued to come. There were arrests and there were spectacular rescues by pro-Abolition crowds. Pro-slavery and anti-slavery crowds fought in the streets and with Northern police. Scarcely a month passed but some escaping slave or ex-slave, avoiding arrest, created a local and sometimes a national agitation.

Slaves on ships revolted against slave-traders and took their ships into port, creating international incidents. Congress was powerless. Ten Northern states legalized their rebelliousness by passing Personal Liberty Laws which protected state officers from arresting fugitive slaves, gave arrested Negroes the right of *habeas corpus* and of trial by jury, and prohibited the use of the jails for runaway Negroes. Long before the basic forces of the nation moved into action for the inevitable showdown the petty bourgeois democrats and revolting slaves had plowed up the land and made the nation irrevocably conscious of the great issues at stake.

The Free Farmers and the Proletariat

Yet neither Negroes nor petty bourgeois democracy were the main force of the second American revolution, and a more extended treatment of American history would make that abundantly clear if that were needed by any serious intelligence. The great battle was over the control of the public domain. Who was to get the land—free farmers or slave owners? The Republican Party, as Commons has said, was not an anti-slavery party. It was a Homestead party. The bloody struggle over Kansas accelerated the strictly political development. Yet it was out of the Abolition movement that flowered the broader political organization of the Liberty Party and the Free Soil Party, which in the middle of the decade finally coalesced into the Republican Party.

It was Marx who pointed out very early (in a letter to Engels, 1 July 1861) that what finally broke down the bourgeois timidity was the great development of the population of free farmers in the Northwest Territory in the decade 1850–60. These free farmers were not prepared to stand any nonsense from the South because they were not going to have the mouth of the Mississippi in the hands of any hostile power. By 1860 the great forces which were finally allied were the democratic petty bourgeoisie, the free farmers in the Northwest, and certain sections of the proletariat. These were the classes that, contrary to 1776, compelled the unwilling bourgeois to lead them. They were the basic forces in the period which led to the revolution. They had to come into action before the battle could be joined. They were the backbone of the struggle.

In all this agitation the proletariat did not play a very prominent role. In New England the working masses were staunch supporters of the movement and the writer has little doubt that when the proletariat comes into its own, further research will reveal, *as it always does*, that the workers played a greater role than is accredited to them. Yet the old question of unemployment, rivalry between the Negroes in the North and the Irish, the latest of the immigrant groups, disrupted one wing of the proletariat. Furthermore, organized labor, while endorsing the Abolitionist movement, was often in conflict with Garrison, who, like Wilberforce in England, was no lover of the labor movement. Organized labor insisted that there was wage slavery as well as Negro slavery, and at times was apt to treat both of them as being on the same level—a monumental and crippling error.

Nevertheless, on the whole, the evidence seems to point to the fact that in many areas the organized proletarian movement, though not in the vanguard, supported the movement for Abolition. Finally, we must guard against one illusion. The Abolition movement dominated the political consciousness of the time. Most Northerners were in sympathy. But few wanted war or a revolution. When people *want* a revolution, they make one. They usually want anything else except a revolution. It was only when the war began that Abolitionists reaped their full reward. Despite all this Abolition sentiment in the North, and particularly in the Northwest areas, the masses of the people on the whole were not anxious to fraternize with the free Negroes, and over large areas there was a distinct hostility. But the free Negroes in the North never allowed this to demoralize them, and the masses of the revolting slaves kept on coming. Between 1830 and 1860, sixty to a hundred thousand slaves came to the North. When they could find no welcome or resting place in the North, some of them went on to Canada. But they never ceased to come. With the Civil War they came in tens and then in hundreds of thousands.

Abolition and the International Proletariat

From its very beginning at the end of the eighteenth century, the Negro struggle for freedom and equality has been an international question. More than that, it seems to be able to exercise an effect, out of all proportion to reasonable expectation, upon people not directly connected with it. In this respect, the Abolition movement in America has curious affinities with the Abolition movement a generation earlier in Britain.

In Britain, before the emancipation in 1832, the industrial bourgeoisie was actively in favor of abolition. It was industrially more mature than the American bourgeoisie in 1850; the West Indian planters were weak, and the slaves were thousands of miles away. But there, too, the earlier Abolition movement assumed a magnitude and importance out of all proportion to the direct interests of the masses who supported it. Earlier, during the French Revolution, the mass revolts of the Negroes brought home to the French people the reality of the conditions which had existed for over a hundred and fifty years. A kind of collective "madness" on the Negro question seemed to seize the population all over France, and no aristocrats were so much hated as the "aristocrats of the skin."

The Abolitionist movement in America found not only a ready audience at home but an overwhelming welcome abroad. Not only did Garrison,

Wendell Phillips, and others lecture in Britain. Frederick Douglass and other Negro Abolitionists travelled over Europe and enrolled many hundreds of thousands in Abolitionist societies. One inspired Negro won seventy thousand signed adherents to the cause in Germany alone. In the decade preceding the Civil War, *Uncle Tom's Cabin* was read by millions in Britain and on the continent, and even as far afield as Italy. And masses of workers and radicals in France, Spain, and Germany took an active interest in the question. Their sentiments bore wonderful fruit during the Civil War itself.

It is not enough to say merely that these workers loved the great American Republic and looked forward to the possibility of emigrating there themselves one day. There are aspects to this question which would repay modern investigation and analysis by Marxists. Charles Beard, who has some insight into social movements in America, is baffled by certain aspects of the Abolition movement. In *Rise of American Civilization*, he writes: "The sources of this remarkable movement are difficult to discover." Much the same can be said of the movement in Britain, which embraced literally millions of people. Thoroughly superficial are the self-satisfied pratings of English historians about the "idealism" of the English as an explanation of the equally baffling Abolition movement in Britain. It would seem that the irrationality of the prejudice against Negroes breeds in revolutionary periods a corresponding intensity of loathing for its practitioners among the great masses of people.*

"The Signal Has Now Been Given"

The slaves played their part to the end. After Lincoln's election and the violent reaction of the South, the North, not for the first time, drew back from Civil War. Congress and the political leaders frantically sought compromise. Frederick Douglass in his autobiography gives an account of the shameful attempts on the part of the North to appease the South. Most of the Northern Legislatures repealed their Personal Liberty Laws. And Douglass concludes his bitter chapter by saying: "Those who may wish to see to what depths of humility and self-abasement a noble people can

---

* It is something for revolutionists to observe in the past and to count on in the future. Already in England, a country where race prejudice is still very strong, the presence of American Negro soldiers, the prejudice against them of white American soldiers, and the reports of Negro upheavals in America have awakened a strong interest among the English masses.

be brought under the sentiment of fear, will find no chapter of history more instructive than that which treats of the events in official circles in Washington during the space between the months of November 1859 and March 1860."

For a long time even Lincoln's stand was doubtful. On December 20, 1860, the very day on which South Carolina seceded, Lincoln made a statement which seemed to exclude compromise. However, in a series of speeches which he delivered on his eleven-day journey to Washington, he confused the nation and demoralized his supporters. Even after the inaugural on March 4, the North as a whole did not know what to expect from him. Marx, as we have seen, had no doubt that the decisive influence was played by the Northwest farmers, who supplied 66 votes, or 36.6 percent, in the college which elected Lincoln.

But there was refusal to compromise from the South also. Says Douglass: "Happily for the cause of human freedom, and for the final unity of the American nation, the South was mad and would listen to no concessions. It would neither accept the terms offered, nor offer others to be accepted."

Why wouldn't they? One reason we can now give with confidence. Wherever the masses moved, there Marx and Engels had their eyes glued like hawks, pens quick to record. On 11 January 1860, in the minds of the critical period described by Douglass, Marx wrote to Engels: "In my opinion the biggest things that are happening in the world today are, on the one hand, the movement of the slaves in America, started by the death of John Brown, and, on the other, the movement of the serfs in Russia. . . . I have just seen in the *Tribune* there has been a fresh rising of slaves in Missouri, naturally suppressed. But the signal now has been given."

Fifteen days later, Engels replied: "Your opinion of the significance of the slave movement in America and Russia is now confirmed. The Harper's Ferry affair with its aftermath in Missouri bears its fruits . . . the planters have hurried their cotton on to the ports in order to guard against any probable consequences arising out of the Harper's Ferry affair." A year later Engels writes to Marx: "Things in North America are also becoming exciting. Matters must be going very badly for them with the slaves if the Southerners dare to play so risky a game."

Eighty years after Marx, a modern student has given details which testify to that unfailing insight into the fundamental processes of historical development, so characteristic of our great predecessors. In Arkansas, in Mississippi, in Virginia, in Kentucky, in Illinois, in Texas, in Alabama, in Northwest Georgia, North Carolina, South Carolina—rebellion and conspiracy swept the South between 1859 and 1860. Writes a contemporary after the John Brown raid: "A most terrible panic, in the meantime, seizes not only the village, the vicinity, and all parts of the state, but every slave state in the Union . . . rumors of insurrection, apprehensions of invasions, whether well founded or ill founded, alter not the proof of the inherent and incurable weakness and insecurity of society, organized upon a slave-holding basis."

The struggle of the Negro masses derives its peculiar intensity from the simple fact that what they are struggling for is not abstract but is always perfectly visible around them. In their instinctive revolutionary efforts for freedom, the escaping slaves had helped powerfully to begin, and now those who remained behind had helped powerfully to conclude, the self-destructive course of the slave power.

THE TWO SIDES OF ABRAHAM LINCOLN (1949)

What is it that the working class must remember about Abraham Lincoln? He himself expressed it best in his second inaugural address when he said of the Civil War:

"Yet, if God wills that it continue until all the wealth piled by the bondman's two hundred and fifty years of unrequited toil shall be sunk, and until every drop of blood drawn with the lash shall be paid by another drawn with the sword, as was said three thousand years ago, so still it must be said, 'The judgements of the Lord are true and righteous altogether.' "

Here was the recognition at last of what the Negroes had done for America, and of what America had done to the Negroes—and the determination at whatever cost to break the power of the reactionary slaveholders. All the chatterers and fakers can be made to turn green and look another way, simply by asking them to explain these words of Lincoln as part of what they call the "democratic process" and "the American way."

Abraham Lincoln was a genuine democrat. When in the Gettysburg address he said "government of the people, by the people, for the people," he meant it. In those days monopoly capital did not exist. A great percentage of the population in the North consisted of small farmers, mechanics, and artisans. It seemed to many men that on the boundless acres that stretched beyond the Mississippi there was room and opportunity for everybody to acquire independence and exercise self-government from the town-meeting to the presidential elections.

But today, with a few giant corporations owning and dominating the economic life of the country and the lives of whole nations abroad; with tens of millions of workers beginning to punch the time-clock at the age of 18 with no other perspective for the rest of their lives until they are thrown out as infirm or incompetent; with the press, radio, and a vast government bureaucracy controlled by a few hundred people, to talk about government "of the people, by the people, for the people" is a mockery and hypocrisy of the worst kind.

Lincoln and others used to say plainly that if the people were dissatisfied with their government it was their revolutionary right to overthrow it. If he had returned and said that on any platform in 1948, Dewey, Truman, Wallace, and Norman Thomas would have united at once to denounce him. The FBI would have tapped his telephone and investigated him. And unmitigated rascals like J. Parnell Thomas and Rankin would have had him up before some House committee and tried to jail him for his "un-Americanism."

Believer in democracy and in the people, determined enemy of the slave-power, from them Lincoln drew the power which made him a great war leader, a writer and speaker whose best efforts will last as long as the English language, a genuine national hero.

Enemy of the slave-power, a friend to the people. That was one side of Lincoln. But there was another which was widely known and commented upon in his own day.

The viciousness of the slave-power, its cruelties and its crimes, its ambition to suppress liberty all over the United States in defense of its precious hordes of slaves, these things were brought and kept before the American people for thirty years by the constant rebellions among the slaves, by the Underground Railroad, and those elements in the North among the whites who supported these revolutionary actions.

Lincoln bitterly opposed all this. He was prepared even as President to use the power of the Federal government to capture and return fugitive slaves.

One of the great chapters in American history is the Abolition movement of Garrison, Phillips, Douglass, and the others who, often hounded, stoned, and beaten, called incessantly for an end to slavery, denouncing it as a crime against civilization and the American people.

Lincoln hated the Abolitionists as trouble-makers, and expressed his approval of their being beaten up.

The formation of the Republican Party was a triumph of the creative power and energy of the American people. Suddenly in 1854 all over the country party units sprang into being and in 1860 it swept into victory. Lincoln had nothing to do with this. Only when it was clear that the Whig Party was doomed did he throw in his lot with the new party.

Not only was Lincoln driven to emancipate the slaves by force of circumstances. He was ready to consider the formation of a Negro republic in Texas. He would have sent all the slaves to Africa if he could have managed it.

Thus with all his virtues he shared to the full the reactionary capitalist prejudices of his day. And it was precisely these that blinded him to the truths which the escaping slaves and the abolitionists taught the American people for thirty years. In the end he had to follow the direction they pointed: civil war, arming of Negroes, crushing of the slave-power.

Lincoln could make these mistakes and still triumph as a leader because John Brown, Garrison, Douglass, and the other had to limit themselves to carrying on a revolutionary propaganda and aiding escaping slaves. Brown's isolated attempt at a slave insurrection was doomed to failure. The workers did not have the numbers, the organization, the social power, the political experience to offer an independent road. The revolutionaries were right as against Lincoln but had no concrete program to place before the country. Thus like Lincoln, when the Republican Party came, they turned to it.

Today we live in an entirely different situation. The enemy is plain: monopoly-capitalism, the modern slave-holders. The class that is to be emancipated is the working class—the workers with the poor farmers and their allies, the great majority of the nation. The party that is to be formed is a great mass party of the proletariat, that will do for American society today what the Republican Party did in 1860–65. The revolutionaries today are those who carry on the traditions of Garrison, Douglass, and John Brown— brutal statement of the facts, refusal to pretend that there is any way out except by the destruction of capitalism, struggle for the independent action of the masses, refusal to compromise on principles. We can do this, and do it better than they did, because we have before our eyes the mighty power of the American proletariat and behind us the great traditions and experiences of Bolshevism.

That is our attitude to Lincoln. . . . We pay him the tribute due to him as a great historical figure, with a place in the struggle for human emancipation.

But for us he is no model. Rather, in the failures of his career and particularly in the men who were so consistently right against him, we find the points of departure to struggle for the unity, not only of North and South, but of all the nations of the world, for the emancipation not only of chattel-slaves but of the vast majority of the peoples of the world, the workers, farmers, and all the exploited and oppressed.

THE 1919 RACE RIOTS IN CHICAGO (1939)

Twenty years ago this summer, there took place the notorious Chicago race riots. They are a good example of how necessary it is to turn our backs on whatever the American bourgeoisie says about the Negroes.

What precisely happened in Chicago twenty years ago? Thousands of Negroes will unsuspectingly give you the account given by Congressman Ellender in the debate on the Anti-Lynching Bill. Many revolutionists—including J. R. Johnson—for years accepted it in outline, and it is probable that many still do, thereby subjecting themselves to the American bourgeoisie.

Mr. Ellender quotes extensively from the World's Work for December 1922, whose version runs as follows.

The great exodus of Negroes from the South created problems of adjustment between whites and blacks, and of course the Negroes were the ones who caused the trouble. They were "illiterate," their manners "uncouth," their clothes "outlandish and bad-smelling." When they found themselves sitting side by side with white people in trolley cars, the Negroes did not know how to behave. They "sprawled in their seats." They insisted on sitting when white women were standing. They went to live in quarters which white immigrants had for years regarded as their own; their children began to mingle in large number with the white children in the schools. But what "caused the greatest ill feeling" was the increasing presence of Negro men and women in the public recreation centers. These impudent Negroes sat in considerable numbers on the park benches, played baseball and basketball on the public fields. They appeared in the municipal dance halls, they shared public bathing beaches with the whites, and, the final crime, "the mere fact that they attended band concerts in large numbers added to the ill-feeling."

Thus was the atmosphere created in which any small incident could and did precipitate a fearful race riot.

Now the natural reaction of a Negro, or a white person who resents white arrogance to Negroes, is to say as follows. If Negroes went to the parks, played baseball and listened to concerts, they were perfectly justified in doing so, and if race riots took place, it was not the Negroes' fault. A liberal would deplore the sad fact and rush to set up an "inter-racial" commission. A revolutionary who was not on his guard would say that here was another example of white workers being dominated by the reactionary ideas of the bourgeoisie. As a matter of fact, such a revolutionary would be himself dominated by bourgeois ideas on the Negro question. Far from being a demonstration of the difficulties of adjustment between white residents and black immigrants, the Chicago race riots are one of the greatest examples of racial solidarity in the whole history of the American working class.

In 1919 there were some 12,000 Negroes working on the stockyards of Chicago. The Stockyards Labor Council, founded in July 1917, had been struggling to organize the industry. The capitalist bosses countered by introducing an increasing number of plants. They hoped to influence the Negroes against the unions, and playing white against black to defeat unionization. The Stockyards Labor Council repudiated the color-line and made a drive to organize the Negroes, for without them the whites could not win. There were inter-racial socials. A Negro was elected Vice-President of the Council. In June 1919, the Council began to organize street-corner meetings of whites and Negroes. This was death for the meat-packing bosses and they used mounted police to break these meetings up. Against this, the Stockyards Labor Council called a protest strike and won, and to celebrate they called a great parade of white and Negro workers in the Negro neighborhood for July 6.

In come the capitalist police and with brazen impudence proclaim that this parade is going to cause racial conflict! They therefore forbid it. The Council, instead of defying the order, made Negroes and whites parade separately, but the two groups met on the Beutner playground at La Salle and 23rd Street and there was grand demonstration of nearly 30,000 Negroes and whites (despite the fact that many of these Negroes had gone to band concerts). The working-class front of black and whites held firm and the capitalists had to break it. So on July 27 they sent whites with faces blackened to look like Negroes who burned a block of houses where white stockyard workers lived. The police followed up this outrage by sending a large force of militia, police, etc, into the stockyards "to prevent racial strife," and agents-provocateurs were let loose among the white workers to incite them to violence.

The Council called a mass meeting of 30,000 white workers which unanimously voted solidarity with the Negroes and demanded that the police withdraw all its armed men from the stockyards. The 4000 Negroes endorsed the vote.

During this period, the riots did take place. Police and their allies, let loose in the Negro district, led the rioting. In their efforts to keep "order," they killed not one white man, but half the Negroes killed met their death at the hands of the police.

Despite this desperate provocation, the 35,000 whites and Negroes in the union remained solid and would not go back to work until the police and militia were removed from the yards. White and black union men worked together to help the wounded. The whites gave financial aid to the Negroes who came to the headquarters for assistance instead of going to the bosses' breadlines. Among 35,000 workers there was only one single case of violence.

The workers black and white had caused the police to be withdrawn from the yards. On the day that they went back there wasn't a single indication of any racial feeling. In one plant, Negroes and Slavs "met as old friends." Many of the men "put their arms around one another's necks." A Negro and a Pole got on a truck and rode all around the plant to show the other workers that a good spirit still existed. Says the official report, "There was nothing in the contact of the Negro or the Pole or the Slav that would indicate that there had ever been a race riot in Chicago, and there was nothing from the beginning of the race riot to the end that would indicate there was any feeling started in the stockyards or in this industry that led to the race riots."

That was twenty years ago. The full story was told in the Stalinist press ten years after, and some of it in official reports. But the bourgeois press and bourgeois publicists still circulate their lies about the Chicago race riots, and with their babble about maladjustment, they cleverly obscure one of the most significant events in American working class history. These lies penetrate even into the revolutionary movement, and will continue to penetrate, unless the revolutionary movement dos not merely content itself with saying "No" to the capitalist "Yes" but turns its back completely on whatever the capitalists say about the Negroes.

Marcus Garvey (1940)

Articles in every newspaper and editorials on Garvey have borne witness to the great impression which this extraordinary man made on American life in less than ten years stay in this country. The revolutionary movement is woodenly obtuse to the immense significance of his career. Thereby it shows itself still dominated by the powerful prejudice which belittles or ignores all action and achievements by Negroes.

Garvey landed in America some time during the war and agitated for his organization, the U.N.I.A., the Universal Negro Improvement Association. He had a fantastic program of Back to Africa, fantastic, because Britain, France, and Germany would not fight wars for Africa and then hand it over to Garvey. It is doubtful whether he believed it himself. It is possible that when he began he took the idea seriously, but before long he must have become convinced of its impracticality. But Garvey's ideas are not important.

The first thing to note is that he burst into prominence in the post-war period, when revolution was raging in Europe and the workers were on the move everywhere. The Negro masses felt the stir of the period, and it was that which made Garvey. The next great movement of the American working class was the pro-Roosevelt movement in 1936. It swung hundreds of thousands of Negro votes from the Republican to the Democratic Party. The third great movement of the American workers was the CIO. It swept hundreds of thousands of Negroes into unions for the first time. In every great step forward of the American masses since the war, the Negroes have played their part. Yet the biggest response was to Garvey.

Why? Garvey was a reactionary. He used fierce words but he was opposed to the labor movement and counseled subservience to bosses. One reason for his success was that his movement was strictly a class movement. He appealed to the black Negroes against the Mulattoes. Thus at one strike he excluded the Negro middle class which is very largely of mixed blood. He deliberately aimed at the poorest, most down-trodden and humiliated Negroes. The millions who followed him, the devotion and the money they contributed, show where we can find the deepest strength of the working class movement, the coiled springs of power which lie there waiting for the party which can unloose them.

Garvey, however, was a race fanatic. His appeal was to black against white. He wanted purity of race. A great part of his propaganda was based on the past achievements of blacks, their present misery, their future greatness.

With that disregard of facts which characterize the born demagogue, he proclaimed there were 400 million Negroes in the world, when there are certainly not half as many. Who does all this remind us of? Who but Adolph Hitler?

The similarity between the two movements does not end there. The Negroes were too few in America for Garvey to give them excitement by means of baiting whites as Hitler baited the Jews. But his program had a nebulousness similar to the the Nazi program. Was this the reason that long before Hitler, he anticipated the Nazi leader in his emphasis on uniforms, parades, military guards, in short, the dramatic and the spectacular? Stupid people saw in all this merely the antics of backward Negroes. Recent events should give them an opportunity to revise their judgements. Everything that Hitler was to do afterwards in the way of psychological appeal, Garvey was doing in 1921. His array of baronets, etc., with himself as Emperor of Africa was a hangover from his early life in the West Indies.

In one important respect, the Garvey movement was the most remarkable political mass movement that America has ever seen. Note that Garvey promised the Negroes nothing and at the same time everything. His organization was not a trade union which offered higher wages, nor was it a political party which could offer prosepcts of realizing a program. All he did was to speak of Africa, and near the end of his career he bought one or two leaky ships which made one or two streaky voyages. Yet so deep was the sense of wrong and humiliation among the Negroes and so high did he lift them up that they gave him all that they did, year after year, expecting Garvey to perform some miracle. No revolution is ever made except when the masses have reached this pitch of exaltation, when they see a vision of a new society. That is what Garvey gave them.

Personally, Garvey was one of the great orators of his time. Ill-educated, but with the rhythms of Shakespeare and the Bible in his head, he was a master of rhetoric and invective, capable of great emotional appeals and dramatic intensity. In his late years he could hold English crowds spellbound in Hyde Park while he told them that God would save black Ethiopia because Simon the Cyrenian, a black man, helped Jesus on the way to Calvary. As the great poet says, it ain't what you say, it's the way that you say it. Yet this remarkable movement and the remarkable figure who led it remain unstudied by American Marxists.

Every two-cent revolutionary who has talked to Negroes in cafeterias and therefore knows the Negro question, points out Garvey's errors and absurdities and thinks that thereby a contribution has been made to knowledge. More than in all the theses of the Comintern, a basis for the building of a real mass movement among the Negroes lies in a thorough study of this first great eruption of the Negro people.

The Communist Party's Zigzags on Negro Policy (1939)

The C.P. passed through three stages in its Negro work: (a) up to 1928 when the Negro work was neglected, (b) 1929–35 when it made a drive, the period of which coincided with the period of [denouncing all other left currents as] social-fascism, and (c) 1935–39, the open abandonment of the revolutionary line by the C.P. and the catastrophic loss of nearly all its Negro membership.

In *The Communist* of September 1929, Cyril Biggs reviews the early experiences of the C.P. on the Negro question. For years, the Negro membership of the C.P. could be counted "literally" on the fingers of one hand. In 1928, the drive was initiated directly by the Comintern, which insisted at the 6th World Congress that the C.P. place the winning of the Negroes as one of its major tasks henceforth in America. The political line of the C.P. in those days was of course the line of social-fascism. Daily they went into action to make the revolution on every street corner. They formed their own red trade unions. They called Roosevelt and the New Dealers the worst enemies of the working class and the initiators of fascism in this country. They foamed at the mouth whenever they mentioned the NAACP and other petty-bourgeois Negro organizations.

That political line was false. It was nearly though not quite as bad as their present line of the Democratic Front—repudiating the revolution, making out Roosevelt and the New Deal to be the sole salvation of the American workers, grinning and smirking at Walter White and the NAACP.

Furthermore in 1929 the C.P. had many blunders to live down. It had opposed the migration of Negroes from the South to the North on the grounds that these newcomers would affect the economic position of the white workers in the North and result in sharpening racial antagonism. The Negro comrades who opposed this "gargantuan stupidity" were refused the five or six dollars they got weekly as postage for the news service they sent out to about 300 Negro newspapers. The C.P. had openly opposed social equality for Negroes at a conception in New York. This piece of stupidity was given wide publicity in the capitalist press and extensively quoted in the Negro press.

Even when the turn was made to the Negroes, the party was guilty of open acts of blatant chauvinism. In the unions there were scores of functionaries and departments for Greek, Italian, Jewish workers etc. But there was not a single Negro functionary, despite the fact that there were several thousand Negro workers in the needle trades in New York City alone. The personal behavior of whites to Negro comrades was frequently such as to damn the party in the minds of all Negroes who heard of it. One Negro comrade, Nicolai Garcia, was in Baltimore six days before he was able to get a bed. The white comrades with whom he came into contact just didn't know what to do with him. Yet two days later when a white comrade arrived from New York and talked about going to a hotel, there were protests and offers from white comrades to put him up. Such incidents always spread like wildfire among Negroes. Here then was a false political line and a party membership many elements of which had not rid themselves of the crudest discrimination and prejudices practiced by capitalist society.

And yet, despite these handicaps, between 1929 and 1936 the party made progress. The social-fascist line at least summoned the masses to struggle. It differentiated sharply between the aims and methods of Communists on the one hand and of bourgeois politicians and vaguely "progressive" persons on the other. The C.P. made a revolutionary approach to the Negroes. And despite distortions of the revolutionary line, the demagogy and corruption, the bureaucratic manipulation of the Negro leaders, the chauvinism open and inverted, the party gained thousands of members and won a sympathetic if critical interest among many sections of the Negro community.

Then the line changed from one that at least attempted to be revolutionary to one which is today openly tied to American imperialism and the Roosevelt war machine. The result was immediate and unmistakable. Of their 2000 Negro members in New York State, the C.P. has lost over 80% and the same thing happened all over the country. . . .

On *The Negro in the Caribbean* by Eric Williams (1943)

The discovery of the West Indies by Christopher Columbus at the end of the fifteenth century speeded the development of the world market and aided in the creation of capitalist society. From that day to this, the islands have been an epitome of capitalist development. The expropriation of the laborers, the rise of commercial capitalism, the transformation to industrial capitalism, the law of uneven development, monopoly capitalism and imperialism; the accumulation of vast capital and vast misery; the necessity for socialism; the growing discipline, unity, and organization of the masses; the proletariat leading the peasantry and preparing unconsciously for the seizure of power; all this, supposed to be a teleology imposed upon historic chaos by Marxian schematism—all this unrolls before us in unbroken sequence in this packed, incisive study by Prof. Eric Williams of Howard University.* It is as if on these islands history had concentrated in tabloid form the story of four hundred years of capitalist civilization.

The evidence is all the more valuable because Williams is no Marxist. But approaching the facts from the point of view of the Negro, i.e. from the point of view of labor, his mastery of his material forces upon him an inevitable pattern, economic necessity, class struggle, etc. He is sure of the past, clear as to the present, but the future demands more than Williams has. It needs a conscious theory. He is a sincere nationalist and a sincere democrat, but after so sure a grasp of historical development as he shows in this history of four centuries, he displays an extreme naivete in his forecasts of the future. He seems to think that the economic forces which have worked in a certain way for four hundred years will somehow cease to work in that way because of the Atlantic Charter and the warblings of Willkie and Wallace. What makes the sudden slide downward so striking is that the whole book is a refutation of just such expectations.

"Capitalism" in Early Agriculture

Williams's method is strictly historical and we shall follow him.

For three centuries the sugar economy and the slave trade dominated the West Indies and the world market. Together they formed the twin foundations of the glory and the greatness of Britain. A few years ago Churchill stated: "Our possession of the West Indies, like that of India . . . gave us the strength, the support, but especially the capital, the wealth, at a time when no other European nation possessed such a reserve which enabled us to come through the great struggles of the Napoleonic Wars, the keen commerce in the eighteenth and nineteenth centuries, and enabled us not only to acquire this appendage of possessions which we have, but also to

* *The Negro in the Caribbean* by Eric Williams. Introduction by Alain Locke.

lay the foundations of that commercial and financial leadership which, when the world was young, when everything outside Europe was undeveloped, enabled us to make our great position in the world." Churchill's words are literally true, and for a considerable period of time those islands were of far greater importance to Britain than the thirteen colonies which later became the United States.

Such is the unevenness of capitalist development. The reason is not generally recognized. It was not because so many people consumed sugar and rum. It was the other way about. Sugar production demanded from the start the application of machinery to raw material on the spot and this soon expanded on a scale far surpassing the application of machinery not only to agriculture but to many contemporary manufacturing processes as well.

The great commerce built up on the slave trade and slavery had its foundations in a very highly advanced and essentially capitalistic mode of production, although this was in the colonies. The Indians were expropriated and the importation of Negroes followed: they were slaves, but slaves in the large-scale production of the factories. Marxism would profit by a study of this highly important phase of capitalist development which Marx did not treat in *Capital*.

Williams does not quite grasp the full economic significance of this phenomenon. Disdaining a clutter of qualifications, he boldly bases his whole thesis on the indisputable fact that: "The black man, emancipated from above by legislation or from below by revolution, remains today the slave of sugar." But he misses the point when he says: "To free the Negro it was necessary not so much to alter the method of production in the sugar industry itself." To alter the method of production! But you could not alter the method of production in 1833, because it was already capitalistic in essence, large-scale production by machinery and production for the world market. Nor could it ever be altered except in one direction: socialism. The French peasant in 1789 could get the land and improve on feudal agriculture. The Russian peasant could get the land and be more or less collectivized. When the West Indian slave was emancipated he found himself free in a highly capitalized agricultural industry. What was to be done with him? On that rock humanitarianism has broken its head for a century, and Williams breaks his also. There has been no further industrialization of any scope to offset, even for a time, this domination by sugar. The sugar problem must be solved in terms of sugar.

Monopoly Capitalism at Work

From their heritage of slavery the islands have never recovered. The capitalistic production not only created a large mass of landless laborers. It made the islands subservient to the one-crop system. It was cheaper for the slave-owner to import food for the slaves, as it is cheaper for the capitalist to import food for the wage-laborers. Thus the slaves starved during the Seven Years War (1756–63) owing to the depredations of the French privateers, just as the workers suffer today owing to the depredations of the German submarines. At the mercy of the capitalist oligarchy, the Negro laborer works sometimes for as little as twenty-five cents a day, three days a week. As in all economies dominated by a single crop, that crop sets the standard of living and the working conditions for all the others.

With the development of imperialism, the West Indian laborers were at the receiving end of this most cruel of all exploitations. In a few years, American finance capital accomplished in Puerto Rico a detestation which had taken centuries in other islands. Ten millions of American dollars are invested in Haiti, 41 millions in the Dominican Republic (three fourths of this in agriculture), 666 millions in Cuban enterprises. Some of these islands are self-governing, such as Cuba; others are plain colonies, such as Puerto Rico, Martinique, and Trinidad. In some, e.g. Jamaica, new agricultural industries, such as the banana industry, have developed. Haiti produces coffee. But over all the islands, taken as a whole, hangs the pall of the sugar industry, now in advanced stages of that world-wide disease, monopoly capitalism.

Helpless before the absentee owners and soulless corporations of London and Wall Street, without democratic rights (until in very recent years he fought for and won a few), the laborer combines in his fate the worst features of capitalist production in its early unregulated days with those of capitalist exploitation in its latest stages unmitigated by progressive legislation, and with the special vices of industry in agriculture. Williams's chapter entitled "The Condition of the Negro Wage Earner" is a masterpiece of compression, a compendium of workers' misery and capitalist callousness marshalled with apparent dispassion but with a suppressed indignation visible between every word. Quotation or abstract is unnecessary. The chapter should be read. Sufficient to say that some fifteen years after America took over the tiny Virgin Islands, 951 of the burials in one year were pauper burials.

The Nature of Imperialist Rivalry

The future of these islands has been complicated by the entry of America as a contender for the islands now owned by Britain and France. The American proletariat thus has a direct interest in their fate. Today, as Lenin pointed out, imperialism has passed beyond the stage of grabbing territory only for the purposes of direct economic exploitation. It grabs for strategic reasons and sometimes for the mere purpose of keeping out other imperialisms. The islands are Britain's last outposts in the New World, invaluable as air bases (both military and commercial) and as ports of call for ships. America wants them for precisely the same reason, and a tenacious undercover struggle is going on for control of these economically bankrupt islands. The Negro wage earner is, for the time being, the focus of imperialist attention. This is why.

In 1937 and 1938 a series of riots broke out in Trinidad, followed by similar revolts in Barbados, Jamaica, and other islands. They were suppressed with great difficulty and the British government sent out two commissions, the Trinidad Commission of 1938–39 under Lord Moyne. The Moyne Commission wrote a report which was suppressed by the British government. Suppression was superfluous. To take one example: in 1897 the Norman Commission (also Royal) had written: "the existence of a class of small proprietors among the population is a source of both economic and political strength." Mayor Wood (now Lord Halifax) had written what amounted to the same in 1922. Lord Oliver had written the same for the Sugar Commission in 1929. Williams does not quote but obviously anticipates the recommendations of the 1938–39 Commission, which have been published. Here is an extract: "The improvement of existing land settlements and the establishment of new settlements." For forty years British commissioners have recommended the break-up of some of the large estates and the settlement of a substantial peasantry. Nothing has been done for the simple reason that the economic and political power is in the hands of the white merchants and the plantation owners. They are supported by the mulatto middle class, which fills the government offices and the professions.

The commissions report, some speeches are made, and then everything goes back to where it was, to become progressively worse. However, in 1937 and 1938, the revolts had been powerful, the people were determined, labor organized itself, and, to complete the awakening, American imperialism demanded and received military bases in Trinidad, Jamaica, and other islands.

The entry of American imperialism accelerated the political development. The Americans saw that defense of islands composed of a population sullenly hostile to the existing government was dangerous from a strictly military point of view. It needed the islands to complete its mastery of North American water and especially in their relations to the Panama Canal. The ruling classes were strongly pro-British and the mulatto middle classes more so, particularly because of their fear of American race prejudice. The Negro masses might be weaned over from Britain. Whereupon, with the report of the Royal Commission still hidden in a closet of British government, Roosevelt appointed yet another commission, this time an Anglo-American commission on which the English personnel once more set out to tour the long-suffering West Indian islands. In Trinidad, one of the American members of the commission stated that the commission had come to repair the economic and social grievances of the West Indian people. The speaker was Rex Tugwell, who is now busy repairing the social and economic ills of West Indians as Governor of Puerto Rico. It seems agreed on all sides that one of the first conditions of repairing Puerto Rican ills is that Rex Tugwell should leave, and should have no American successor. Meanwhile the BBC bombards the island nightly with propaganda and OWI does the same for Washington, in propaganda which subtly aims at making the masses feel that they will at last get some redress of their wrongs from America. With such a base established, America can then give Britain the works. Thus the "United" Nations.

Imperialist Bankruptcy

In reality, imperialism, of whatever stamp, short of abolishing itself, can do nothing except grudgingly subsidize these islands. On a few pages Williams tackles the fundamental problem of the Caribbean, the Negro wage earner's future. Is his future peasant proprietorship? Williams gives arguments to show that as far as the production of the sugar cane is concerned, peasant proprietorship has not been proved to be economically less productive than large-scale ownership. In his admirable articles on Puerto Rico in *Labor Action*, V. Segundo has tackled the same problem.

The writer of the present article has for many years carefully studied contradictory arguments by learned economists and tendentious politicians on this question, and can here merely state his own considered opinion.

The break-up of the large estates would be economically a reactionary step, i.e., in its historical sense. But the political class relation, the needs of the masses, require another yardstick. If the masses want land, then they should have the right to decide and break up the estates. The economically progressive growth of large-scale production has been characteristic of sugar production in the West Indies from its very inception. What is needed is expropriation of the sugar proprietors and absentee landlords and capitalists and collective production by the laborers themselves—in other words, the socialist revolution. It will be the task of Marxists patiently to explain, if it is at all necessary, the economic superiority of large-scale production.

Williams agrees that whatever reorganization takes place internally, the fate of West Indian sugar depends upon the world market. But without the socialist revolution in Europe and America the world market will still be the world market of old, dominated by American imperialism. Against that monstrous octopus, the West Indian laborer will be, as he has always been, the miserable victim of a power which will continue to grind the life out of him as mercilessly as the mills grind the juice from the cane. That, as Williams so conclusively shows, has been his fate for four hundred years. What reason is there to think that without a revolution there will be any change? Williams's whole book refutes the possibility of any such peaceful change. If America takes over, the laborer will change masters. That's all. Puerto Rico is the proof.

The Proletariat Takes Charge

Is the idea of socialist revolution for these islands remote? No more than elsewhere; in fact, it is nearer there than for many other places. The recent history of these islands shows this.

In 1938 Ormsby Gore reviewed the colonial empire in the House of Commons on the single day allotted per year to this task by that "demo-cratic" body. He stated that $110,000 had been spent on land settlement in Jamaica. One weekend, some months after, the Colonial office received a cabled message from the Governor of Jamaica, Sir Edward Denham. It was an urgent message, for the British officials interrupted their indispens-able weekend. They cabled back to Sir Edward that he was to announce immediately to the Jamaican people that the sum of two and a half *million* dollars would be appropriated for land settlement. The excitement was too much for Sir Edward and he died that very weekend. The report is that his stomach tied up into a knot. Well it might. The stomach of West Indian Governor is usually much more pleasantly employed than in trying to digest a mass revolt of the Jamaican people.

The series of revolts in both Jamaica and Trinidad began with organized labor, the dock workers in Jamaica and the oil workers in Trinidad. Thence they spread to the population. In Trinidad the strike was general and lasted fourteen days. Though the people are not yet thinking in terms of socialism, they are travelling fast. Labor has organized trade unions and formed a trade union federation in certain islands. In Trinidad and Jamaica, national parties have been formed which are pledged to national independence. The Jamaican stevedore union, which led the revolt there, was stimulated and materially aided by the sailors of the American Maritime Union. When British troops landed in Trinidad in 1937 some of them told the people: "Go ahead. We don't want to shoot you." The people now have a passionate interest in foreign affairs and in the history of the trade union and labor movement abroad.

The stay-in strike in Trinidad in 1937 was directly inspired by the sit-down strikes in America which ushered in the CIO. The British, blind as only the doomed are blind, fought to retain all possible political power. But in the fall of 1942 the British Under Secretary of State for the Colonies visited Washington. At this gentleman's press conference, Roosevelt, who sat with him, declared himself to be in favor not only of compulsory education but of universal suffrage for the West Indies. Caught between the revolting masses and the rival imperialism, the British in February 1943 "granted" universal suffrage to one small island, Jamaica. On the ground that the laborers were not yet fit for this, they had opposed the measure for 25 years. And now Roosevelt would get the credit. Roosevelt, on the other hand, after the typical British fashion, carefully explains to Puerto Ricans that they are not yet fit for their demands. Even in Jamaica the concession, extorted at the point of the bayonet, so to speak, has only whetted the political appetite.

In Puerto Rico, in Jamaica, in Trinidad, in Barbados, behind all the complicated forms and stages of constitutions, the imperialist Governor governs in the interests of imperialism and its local representatives. The West Indian masses today know this and are determined to put an end to it. They need all the help they can get. And none so deserve help. During the last six years they have travelled further politically and organizationally than they did in the whole century since emancipation. This they have done practically unaided, being swept into the current of the modern proletarian movement by their suffering at the hands of capitalism at home and the chaos of capitalism abroad. This much is certain: that is soon as the proletariat of America, in particular, gives them the signal, they will seize power and put an end to the economic system which has choked them for so long. With increasing political power and labor organization, they have great battles ahead of them. They may even find it necessary to create peasant proprietors, and would be most eminently justified in demanding large subsidies for the purpose from the people who have leached away their lifeblood for so many generations.

It is precisely by vigorous struggle for immediate needs that they have progressed so far, and the same course followed, in coordination with labor abroad, will ultimately bring them inevitably to the struggle for social- ist power. Capitalism will see to that. Williams's immediate demands— federation, national independence, political democracy—are admirable, but he commits a grave error in thinking, as he obviously does, that these will end or even seriously improve West Indian mass poverty and decay. But for this lapse, his book is a little triumph, admirably planned and very well written. It should be read not only by those specially interested in the Negro problem or the West Indies. It is in its bourgeois way a short but instructive study of capitalist beginnings, maturity, decline; and, most important today, of the way in which it generates, out of is its own bosom, the forces which are to destroy it.

KEY PROBLEMS IN THE STUDY
OF NEGRO HISTORY (1950)

The writers and organizer of the study of Negro history have reached a critical stage in their work. They have accumulated an imposing body of facts which demonstrate the active participation of Negroes in the making of American history and, in particular, in the creation of the American liberal and revolutionary tradition. It is today impossible to write a serious history of the Civil War period without taking into consideration the research which has gone into the making of the *Journal of Negro History*.

But what next? Merely to go on accumulating facts? Obviously that is not sufficient. Benjamin Quarles' study of Frederick Douglass shows the dilemma. This careful, conscientious Negro scholar, after years of study, simply could not come to any definitive conclusion about the significance of the career of Douglass; he sought the secret of Douglass in Douglass' personal character, selfishness, ambition. Yet the truth is that no single individual so embodied in himself the growth and development of the social forces in America which brought the North-South conflict to a head.

After the election of 1860, Lincoln and the bourgeoisie took over. But until that time, Douglass as the slave who escaped, as the brilliant lieutenant of Garrison and Phillips, and then as the man who broke with them to urge political action, without giving up his principles as a radical abolitionist— Douglass is the most symbolical figure of the pre-Civil War period. Yet after all the work the Negro historians have done on him, his significance, both as an American and as an American Negro, eludes them.

It eludes them because historical facts, as facts, can do so much and no more. They have to be organized in the light of a philosophy of history. To be quite precise, they have to be consciously organized in the light of a correct philosophy of history. For whether a writer knows it or not, he is always using a philosophy of history. In the case of American historical writers, it is the philosophy of liberalism and parliamentary democracy. Because they resented the lies and ignorance about Negroes which this philosophy produced, the Negroes went to the archives and produced the facts which have altered the general conceptions regarding the part played by Negroes in the U.S. But while recognizing that the "democratic" conception of the Beards, Hackers, and Schlessingers is inadequate, they have not been able to substitute any other historical method for it.

Their dilemma is not at all a Negro one. It affects the writing of history from one end of the world to another, and nowhere more sharply than in the history of revolutionary periods such as the English Civil War of the 17th century, the French revolution of the 18th century, and the Russian revolution of this century. All these great historical events are in process of re-evaluation, like the Civil War in the U.S., with regard to the same problem.

It has been estimated that in France there are more books on the great period of the French revolution (1789–94) than on all the rest of French history. Yet when Daniel Guerin recently published his history of that period, he was able to raise so many fundamental questions, illuminate so many obscure ones, and throw so much confusion into accepted theories, that friends and enemies alike had to agree that a new stage had been reached.

Why? Because Guerin, a revolutionary socialist, for the first time posed unambiguously and in the most militant fashion the role of the artisans, workers, and peasants in the French revolution, bringing them and their leaders like Variet, Rous, and Leclerc, hitherto generally neglected for the historically famous Dantons and Robespierres, into the very center of his investigations of the causes and course of the revolution.

The same thing has happened in regard to the Puritan revolution in Britain. The Levellers and men like John Lilburne, from being mere footnotes to history, have become the center of important studies in both England and America; the historical dominance of men like Oliver Cromwell has been seriously challenged, and here, as in France, the role of the masses is the center of attention.

In Russia the same problem has taken an entirely opposite turn. Stalin and the Kremlin, oppressors of the people, have rewritten the history of the Russian revolution, excluded the role of Trotsky and all who opposed their bureaucratic oppression of the people, and through their Communist parties have spent millions in trying to impose upon the people of the world a version of the Russian revolution which makes the whole mighty development the result of the wisdom, foresight, energy, and courage of Stalin. Among the many reasons why they hate Trotskyism so bitterly is that it has exposed these falsifications at every opportunity.

It is not hard to understand why this theoretical battle over the role played by the masses in past revolutions assumes such importance. Not merely because of the past, but because one of the problems in the contemporary world is: Can the people, the workers, the peasants, the lower middle class, use their immense power to reorganize a collapsing society and at the same time not fall under the grip of totalitarianism?

The Negro historians have not as a whole faced this question. They first sought to rely on the facts alone. Where they did begin to study historical method, they fell under the influence of the Stalinists. But all Stalinist history, following the great example of their masters in Russia, pays lip service to the role of the masses while in reality sparing no pains to exalt the ideas of submission, discipline, authority. They do not point out the importance of leaders as men who have worked with the masses for years, as men whom the masses know and trust, as men whose every step is conditioned by recognition of the fact that they represent the deepest instincts and desires of the mass. Not at all. The conception they seek to inculcate is the conception of authority, the kind of authority the dictators of the Kremlin wield, the kind of authority that the CP leadership seeks to establish over the working class movement in every country.

Because of the demagogy, skill, and historical doubletalk with which the Stalinists cover their tracks, it has taken a long time for the Negro writers to recognize that what the Stalinists parade as "Marxism" leads them nowhere.

What is the way out? The Negro writers have to pose and grapple with the general historical question: What is the role of the masses in great revolutionary upheavals? They will find that instead of dealing, as they have been doing, with the Negro's role in U.S. history, they are dealing with a world-wide problem of historical writings which is engaging the attention of serious historians today as never before.

Once they have grappled with what modern writers are saying about the role of the mass movements in the English and French revolutions, once they master directly what Marx and Engels had to say about these revolutions and what Lenin and Trotsky had to say about the Russian Revolution, they will find that the role of the Negro masses and Negro political leaders will begin to fall into well-defined political patterns. They will have to tackle the Stalinist corruption at its source. They will have to study Trotsky's *History of the Russian Revolution* and, side by side with it, the versions of the Stalinist historians. They will have to study Stalinist accounts of the rise of Stalinism, and Trotsky's *Stalin*. They will have to study and to decide.

Until then they will continue, as they are doing now, to accumulate material but be unable to make use of it; not only that, they will not be able to hold even the positions they have now. Already liberal historians like Nevins are backing a counter-attack with attempts to show that the Civil War was not fought over slavery as an economic system but was a moral question. The Stalinist Aptheker now promises to show that it was the poor whites in the South who initiated the struggle for freedom from slavery.

The Negro writers on Negro history therefore have to make a big step forward. But having made it they will find that they will add great contributions, not only to American history, but to world history. Their work will be drawn into what is already a movement on a world scale. They will begin to reap the full fruits of their patient, pioneering work.

They will also find that if they do this work as it ought to be done they will be led to the solution not merely of historical problems but of the burning political questions of the day—the future of the U.S. as well as of the Negro people. For history is a part of the class struggle.

In their determination to right the wrongs done to Negroes, the writers of Negro history have done much to clear away the jungle of lies and falsehoods which obscured American history whenever it approached Negroes. Now the time has come to link that work deliberately and consciously with the most progressive historical currents of the day. A heavy price will inevitably be paid if this is not done.

SIX

Aspects of Marxist Theory

LENIN ON AGRICULTURE AND THE NEGRO QUESTION (1947)

It is remarkable but not strange that the great leaders of Marxist thought—Marx, Engels, Lenin, and Trotsky—all took the keenest interest in the Negro question in the United States. The interest of Marx and Engels centered chiefly on the Civil War. They insisted from the start that the issue at stake was slavery. Trotsky always had a passionate interest in the Negro question, and this increased when he came to live in Mexico. Of the four, the one who seemed most remote from the problem was Lenin. Yet in one of his lesser known writings, he showed his interest in and knowledge of the problem.

The work itself is not that easy to read. It is entitled *Capitalism in Agriculture* and appeared in the very last volume of his *Selected Works* (in English). The origin of this work is interesting and significant.

Lenin had been carrying on for years a controversy with those who were attacking Marx's analysis of the influence of capital on agriculture. This was no mere "theoretical" discussion with him—nor, for that matter, with them either. The driving force of the Russian Revolution was the agricultural question. Lenin insisted that the penetration of capital into the Russian countryside was creating a social differentiation among the peasants, disrupting the traditional relations. He particularly emphasized this disruption: the creation of wealthy tenant-farmers and owners on the one hand and, on the other hand, of poor farmers who worked for wages a few days of the week.

Needless to say, in this disruption Lenin saw the growing basis of revolutionary struggle. His opponents of all stripes argued in various forms the specifically Russian thesis that the old communal life of the peasants provided a basis for some special type of Russian socialism. This would avoid the antagonism between capital and labor, which terrified them with its prospect of inevitable revolution.

It is characteristic of the methods of Bolshevism that Lenin gave his opponents no rest. However remote and semi-scientific their theories might be, he dragged their ideas out into the open and exposed their counter-revolutionary implications. In pursuit of these attackers of Marx and enemies of revolution, Lenin embarked on a study of capitalism in *American* agriculture. He made a close examination and study of the American census of 1910 and wrote his findings in one of the most solid studies of capitalism in agriculture that it is possible to read. In the course of this study, he had occasion to deal with the Negro question.

Lenin separated the South from the rest of the United States, which he further divided into the highly organized individual farming of the New England states, and the farming of the broad acres in the middle West. And in his analysis of Southern farming, he paid special attention to the Negro question.

His analysis can be summarized as follows. The abolition of slavery did not entirely abolish all traces of the old chattel slavery. They remained in the subordination, the degradation, the inhuman conditions of labor of the Negroes. He details the number of tenant farmers, their increasing decay, their poverty and misery; and he laid special emphasis on the fact that this tendency was bound to increase.

Lenin did not write only from analysis of figures and of his reading. As his other writings show, he had observed and studied a very similar phenomenon in Russia. The American slaves had been freed in 1863. The serfs in Russia were emancipated in 1864. But despite the emancipation, many of the old feudal conditions had persisted. In his analysis of conditions in the South among the Negroes, Lenin pointed out that the remains of feudalism in Russia and of chattel slavery in the United States were much the same. He knew the situation of the small tenant and the sharecropper in Russia on which he had repeatedly written in the past. He recognized similar conditions among the Negroes in the United States.

As a matter of fact, what is quite revealing is that Lenin, in his writings on the social conditions in Russia, lays heavy emphasis on the personal tyranny exercised by the landlord over the Russian sharecropper. And after analyzing statistically the situation of the Southern Negro, he writes as one who knows. One can imagine the situation of people who live in those economic and social conditions.

It would take too long here, in this column, to point out the highly instructive parallels between the similar results of a certain economic system even in countries as widely different as Czarist Russia and the U.S. The point is that Lenin, in his unwearying task of educating the Russian proletariat, made analyses and observations of the Negroes in Southern agriculture which are of permanent value to us today, over thirty years afterward.

A great revolution in Russia destroyed that particular agrarian tyranny. In the U.S. the tyranny still continues, though under different conditions. Yet the basic pattern is the same today as it was when Lenin wrote in 1913. We can say categorically that it is impossible to get a real grasp of the social classes in the agricultural South and their development during the past fifty years without a close study of Lenin's analysis of Southern agriculture, and his brief but pregnant presentation of the Negro question.

FROM THE MASTER-SLAVE DIALECTIC TO REVOLT IN CAPITALIST PRODUCTION (1946)

In *The Phenomenology of Mind* (one of the three basic books used by Lenin in his studies for *Imperialism*), in the section on Lordship and Bondage, Hegel shows that the lord has a desire for the object and enjoys it. But because he does not actually work on it, his desire lacks objectivity. The labor of the bondman, in working, in changing, i.e. in negating the raw material, has the contrary effect. This, his *labor*, gives him his rudimentary sense of personality. Marx hailed this and continued the basic idea in his analysis of handicraft and the early stages of capitalist production (simple co-operation). The laborer's physical and mental faculties are developed by the fact that he makes a whole chair, a whole table, a piece of armor, or a whole shoe.

With the development of the stage of manufacture, however, there begins the division of labor, and here instead of making one object, man begins to produce fragments of an object. *In the process of production*, there begins stultification, distortion, and ossification of his physical and intellectual faculties.

With the productive process of heavy industry, this stultification is pushed to its ultimate limit. Man becomes merely an appendage to a machine. He no longer uses the instruments of production. As Marx repeats on page after page, the instruments of production use him. Hegel, who had caught hold of this, was completely baffled by it and, seeing no way out, took refuge in idealism. Marx, using the Hegelian method and remaining in the productive process itself, discovered and elaborated one of the most profound truths of social and political psychology. In the very degradation of the workers he saw the basis of their emancipation. Attacking Proudhon in *The Poverty of Philosophy* (1847) for misunderstanding dialectic, he wrote of the laborer in the automatic factory: "But from the moment that all special development ceases, the need of universality, the tendency towards an integral development of the individual, begins to make itself felt." This need of the individual for universality, for a sense of integration so powerful among all modern oppressed classes, is the key to vast areas of social and political jungles of today. The fascists, for example, understood it thoroughly.

Twenty years later, in *Capital*, Marx developed the political results of the argument in full. "It is as a result of the division of labor in manufactures, that the laborer is brought face to face with the intellectual potencies of the material process of production as the property of another and as a ruling power." He does not need revolutionary parties to teach him this. [The labor process] is his revolutionary education. It begins in manufacture. "It is complete in modern industry . . . ." This is the misery that is accumulated as capital is accumulated. It may not be formulated. But the moment bourgeois society breaks down and the worker breaks out in insurrection, for whatever incidental purpose, resentment against the whole system explodes with terrible power.

The babblers who think that all the American workers want is "full employment" are in for a rude awakening. That capitalism increases the use-values (radio, education, books, etc) that he uses outside of production only increases his antagonism.

The educational process is not individual but social. As Marx insisted and Lenin never wearied in pointing out, in addition to this personal, individual education, capital educates the worker socially and politically. In *Capital*,

Marx quoted a passage he had written twenty years before in the *Manifesto*. Former systems, all of them, aimed at conservation of the existing mode of production. Far different is capital:

> Constant revolution in production, uninterrupted disturbances of all social conditions, ever-lasting uncertainty and agitation, distinguish the bourgeois epoch from all earlier ones. All fixed, fast-frozen prejudices, with their train of ancient and venerable prejudices and opinions are swept away, all new formed ones become antiquated before they can ossify. All that is solid melts into air, all that is holy is profaned, and man is at last compelled to face with sober senses his real conditions of life, and his relations with his kind.

. . . . The very climax of Marx's chapter on "The General Law of Capitalist Accumulation" is the warning that "This antagonistic character of capitalist accumulation is enunciated in varied forms by political economists, although by them it is confounded with phenomena, certainly to some extent analogous but nevertheless essentially distinct and belonging to pre-capitalist modes of production," i.e. the Middle Ages. And why essentially distinct? Because in capital alone the degradation and its historical conditions also create in the workers the determination to overthrow the system and acquire for themselves the intellectual potencies of the material process of production.

CAPITALISM AND THE WELFARE STATE (1950)

Negroes have arrived where they are in the United States, and the Welfare State of U.S. capitalism is what it is, because of certain fundamental laws of capitalist development. Nowhere are they so superbly stated as in the famous Chapter XXI of Marx's *Capital* entitled "The Historical Tendency of Capitalist Accumulation." There Marx recapitulates the great law of centralization and its result in economic and social life. Capitalism tends inevitably to become a system of social, i.e. mass production. There develops "on an ever increasing scale, the cooperative form of the labor process, the conscious technical application of science, the methodical cultivation of the soil, the transformation of the instruments of labor into instruments of labor only usable in common, the economizing of all means of production by their use as the means of production of combined, socialized labor, the entanglement of all peoples in the net of the world market, and with this, the international character of the capitalist regime."

This is the movement which formed the industrial concentrations of Detroit, Pittsburgh, Chicago, Youngstown, Los Angeles. This is the movement which, in periods of economic expansion such as the two world wars, brought millions of Negroes from the South and knit them into industrial units with whites. The Negroes became part of the vast cooperative social process of production. This is the ever-extending basis of a potential socialist society, *created by capitalism itself*. But capitalism reigns and by every effort in its power holds on to its control of the economy and the government, and all its perquisites such as the housing system it has developed. Thus arises a violent conflict between the progressive movement of the proletariat in production and the attempt of the capitalists to exploit that movement for their own benefit. So Marx continues: "Along with the constantly diminishing number of the magnates of capital, who usurp and monopolize all advantages of this process of transformation, grows the mass of misery, oppression, slavery, degradation, exploitation."

This is precisely what happens in every sphere of capitalist society and what is happening to the Negroes. Never have Negroes felt so keenly the misery, oppression, slavery and degradation of capitalism. But with their numbers in industry increasing, joining the union, gaining confidence, strength, and solidarity with white workers, they react with increasing violence against their conditions of life and labor. This, too, is an expression of Marx's law that, if the mass of misery, oppression, slavery, degradation, exploitation grows, "with this too grows the revolt of the working class, a class always increasing in numbers and discipline, united, organized by the very mechanism of the process of production itself."

This, in brief, is the Marxist analysis of modern historical development, The instruments of labor only usable in common, huge factories, means of transport covering the whole country, vast organizations for the distribution of goods, services and information, a disciplined, united, organized working class, constantly incorporating Negroes into this discipline, unity and organization, the internationalization of production and society—all these are the premises and preparations for a new mode of production, and for corresponding new forms of housing, education, etc.

But these new forms of life and work can be attained only through the struggle for a socialist society. Meanwhile this new form of society is being suppressed, thwarted, choked, retarded, by the old capitalist order inside and outside of production. Until this basic conflict is resolved, the crises will continue. The ultimate end must be either socialism or the descent into totalitarian barbarism.

That is the stage we have reached. And that is the stage which has produced the Welfare State to defend the old outlived system against the advances in the new. Despite its attack on the Welfare State, the Republican Party has nothing to offer but a promise to administer the Welfare State more cheaply. It is no more than another defender of capitalism. The working class, which grows continuously in numbers, in discipline, in unity, in organization, revolts more and more bitterly and effectively against the degradation and exploitation of capitalism. The more oppressed sections of society, conscious of the protection given by a militant labor movement, raise their special grievances. A general and growing movement for the reorganization of society develops. Other sections of society, stirred by the prevailing social disruption, take up the cause of the oppressed.

In America no cause is so obviously just and crying for amelioration as the cause of the Negroes. Hence the tremendous support given to the Negro cause by millions who are not in the labor movement. Under these circumstances, the capitalist class can try fascism as it did in Germany, which involves the total suppression of organized labor, and, once that is accomplished, the brutal molding and streamlining of the old capitalist system to meet the needs of monopoly capitalism threatened by socialism. But fascism (for the time being) has sustained great defeats on a world scale and is now in discredit. Hence (for the time being) the resort to the demagogy of the Welfare State.

Is it then futile to fight for the passage of civil rights legislation and to demand that Truman live up to his promises? Not at all! Conducted vigorously and without illusions, the struggle for anti-discrimination legislation is a highly progressive struggle, both for its immediate aims and its results. Negro persecution will fall only with the fall of capitalism. But that can take place only when the vast majority of the population realizes that the Welfare State provides no solutions to their problems.

To defeat the opponents of anti-Jim Crow legislation would be a great victory for the Negroes and the whole American people: a field chosen, the issue posed, and the enemy defeated. But after this victory, the workers, Negroes, and all who feel only the blows and get none of the advantages of capitalism, would inevitably confront another side of the Welfare State.

President Truman in his interview with Arthur Krock of the *New York Times* has already warned that if legislation which seeks to compel employers to hire Negroes is passed, he would not administer it. Good. Let him not only say so, but let him do so, for all the world to see. Hard and bitter as that experience would be, there is no other road for the social development of this great country and the political education of its masses.

The Negroes are furthest ahead in the growing comprehension of the true nature of the Welfare State. They, therefore, have a duty to themselves, to the country, to the world. They must show by the presentation of their own irrefutable experience that the Welfare State is not the friend but the double-edged enemy and deceiver of the Negro people and the world at large. . . .

SEVEN

After Ten Years

The decay of capitalism on a world scale, the rise of the CIO in the United States, and the struggle of the Negro people, have precipitated a tremendous battle for the minds of the Negro people and for the minds of the population in the US as a whole over the Negro question. During the last few years certain sections of the bourgeoisie, recognizing the importance of this question, have made a powerful theoretical demonstration of their position, which has appeared in *The American Dilemma* by Gunnar Myrdal, a publication that took a quarter of a million dollars to produce. Certain sections of the sentimental petty bourgeoisie have produced their spokesmen, one of whom is Lillian Smith. That has produced some very strange fruit, which however has resulted in a book which has sold some half a million copies over the last year or two. The Negro petty bourgeoisie, radical and concerned with Communism, has also made its bid in the person of Richard Wright, whose books have sold over a million copies. When books on such a controversial question as the Negro question reach the stage of selling half a million copies it means that they have left the sphere of literature and have now reached the sphere of politics.

We can compare what we have to say that is new by comparing it to previous positions on the Negro question in the socialist movement. The proletariat, as we know, must lead the struggles of all the oppressed and all those who are persecuted by capitalism. But this has been interpreted in the past—and by some very good socialists too—in the following sense: the independent struggles of the Negro people have not got much more than an episodic value and, as a matter of fact, can constitute a great danger not only to the Negroes themselves, but to the organized labor movement. The real leadership of the Negro struggle must rest in the hands of organized labor and of the Marxist party. Without that the Negro struggle is not only weak, but is likely to cause difficulties for the Negroes and dangers to organized labor. This, as I say, is the position held by many socialists in the past. Some great socialists in the United States have been associated with this attitude.

We, on the other had, say something entirely different.

We say, number one, that the Negro struggle, the independent Negro struggle, has a vitality and a validity of its own; that it has deep historic roots in the past of America and in present struggles; it has an organic political perspective, along which it is travelling, to one degree or another, and everything shows that at the present time it is travelling with great speed and vigor.

We say, number two, that this independent Negro movement is able to intervene with terrific force upon the general social and political life of the nation, despite the fact that it is waged under the banner of democratic rights, and is not led necessarily either by the organized labor movement or the Marxist party. We say, number three, and this is the most important, that it is able to exercise a powerful influence upon the revolutionary proletariat, that it has got a great contribution to make to the development of the proletariat in the United States, and that it is in itself a constituent part of the struggle for socialism. In this way we challenge directly any attempt to subordinate or to push to the rear the social and political significance of the independent Negro struggle for democratic rights. That is our position. It was the position of Lenin thirty years ago. It was the position of Trotsky which he fought for during many years. It has been concretized by the general class struggle in the United States, and the tremendous struggles of the Negro people. It has been sharpened and refined by political controversy in our movement, and best of all it has had the benefit of three or four years of practical application in the Negro struggle and in the class struggle by the Socialist Workers' Party during the past few years.

Now if this position has reached the stage where we can put it forward in the shape that we propose, that means that to understand it should be by now simpler than before; and by merely observing the Negro question, the Negro people, rather, the struggles they have carried on, their ideas, we are able to see the roots of this position in a way that was difficult to see ten or even fifteen years ago. The Negro people, we say, on the basis of their own experiences, approach the conclusions of Marxism. And I will have briefly to illustrate this as has been shown in the Resolution.

First of all, on the question of imperialist war. The Negro people do not believe that the last two wars, and the one that may overtake us, are a result of the need to struggle for democracy, for freedom of the persecuted peoples by the American bourgeoisie. They cannot believe that.

On the question of the state, what Negro, particularly below the Mason-Dixon line, believes that the bourgeois state is a state above all classes, serving the needs of all the people? They may not formulate their belief in Marxist terms, but their experience drives them to reject this shibboleth of bourgeois democracy.

On the question of what is called the democratic process, the Negroes do not believe that grievances, difficulties of sections of the population, are solved by discussions, by voting, by telegrams to Congress, by what is known as the "American way."

Finally, on the question of political action, the American bourgeoisie preaches that Providence in its divine wisdom has decreed that there should be two political parties in the United States, not one, not three, not four, just two: and also in its kindness, Providence has shown that these two parties should be one, the Democratic Party and the other, the Republican, to last from now until the end of time.

That is being challenged by increasing numbers of people in the United States. But the Negroes more than ever have shown it—and any knowledge of their press and their activities tells us that they are willing to make the break completely with that conception.

As Bolsheviks we are jealous, not only theoretically but practically, of the primary role of the organized labor movement in all fundamental struggles against capitalism. That is why for many years in the past this position on the Negro question has had some difficulty in finding itself thoroughly accepted, particularly in the revolutionary movement, because there is this difficulty—what is the relation between this movement and the primary role of the proletariat—particularly because so many Negroes, and most disciplined, hardened, trained, highly developed sections of the Negroes, are today in the organized labor movement.

First the Negro struggles in the South are not merely a question of struggles of Negroes, important as those are. It is a question of the reorganization of the whole agricultural system in the United States, and therefore a matter for the proletarian revolution and the reorganization of society on socialist foundations.

Secondly, we say in the South that although the embryonic unity of whites and Negroes in the labor movement may seem small and there are difficulties in the unions, yet such is the decay of Southern society and such the fundamental significance of the proletariat, particularly when organized in labor unions, that this small movement is bound to play the decisive part in the revolutionary struggles that are inevitable.

Thirdly, there are one and a quarter million Negroes, at least, in the organized labor movement.

On these fundamental positions we do not move one inch. Not only do we not move, we strengthen them. But there still remains in question: what is the relationship of the independent Negro mass movement to the organized labor movement? And here we come immediately to what has been and will be a very puzzling feature unless we have our basic position clear.

Those who believed that the Negro question is in reality, purely and simply, or to a decisive extent, merely a class question, pointed with glee to the tremendous growth of the Negro personnel in the organized labor movement. It grew in a few years from three hundred thousand to one million; it is now one and a half million. But to their surprise, instead of this lessening and weakening the struggle of the independent Negro movement, *the more the Negroes went into the labor movement, the more capitalism incorporated them into industry, the more they were accepted in the union movement. It is during that period, since 1940, that the independent mass movement has broken out with a force greater than it has ever shown before.*

That is the problem that we have to face, that we have to grasp. We cannot move forward and we cannot explain ourselves unless we have it clearly. And I know there is difficulty with it. I intend to spend some time on it, because if that is settled, all is settled. The other difficulties are incidental. If, however, this one is not clear, then we shall continually be facing difficulties which we shall doubtless solve in time.

Now Lenin has handled this problem and in the Resolution we have quoted him. He says that the dialectic of history is such that small independent nations, small nationalities, which are powerless—get the word, please—*powerless*, in the struggle against imperialism *nevertheless* can act as one of the ferments, one of the bacilli, which can bring on to the scene the real power against imperialism—the socialist proletariat.

Let me repeat it please. Small groups, nations, nationalities, themselves powerless against imperialism, nevertheless can act as one of the ferments, one of the bacilli which will bring on to the scene the real fundamental force against capitalism—the socialist proletariat.

In other words, as so often happens from the Marxist point of view from the point of view of the dialectic, this question of the *leadership* is very complicated.

What Lenin is saying is that although the fundamental force is the proletariat, although these groups are powerless, although the proletariat has got to lead them, it does not by any means follow that they cannot do anything until the proletariat actually comes forward to lead them. *He says exactly the opposite is the case.*

They, by their agitation, resistance and the political developments that they can initiate, can be the means whereby the proletariat is brought on to the scene.

Not always, and every time, not the sole means, but one of the means. That is what we have to get clear.

Now it is very well to see it from the point of view of Marxism which developed these ideas upon the basis of European and Oriental experiences. Lenin and Trotsky applied this principle to the Negro question in the United States. What *we* have to do is to make it concrete, and one of the best means of doing so is to dig into the history of the Negro people in the United States, and to see the relationship that has developed between them and revolutionary elements in past revolutionary struggles.

For us the center must be the Civil War in the United States and I intend briefly now to make some sharp conclusions and see if they can help us arrive at a clearer perspective. Not for historical knowledge, but to watch the movement as it develops before us, helping us to arrive at a clearer perspective as to this difficult relationship between the independent Negro movement and the revolutionary proletariat. The Civil War was a conflict between the revolutionary bourgeoisie and the Southern plantocracy. That we know. That conflict was inevitable. But for twenty to twenty-five years before the Civil War actually broke out, the masses of the Negroes in the South, through the underground railroad, through revolts, as Aptheker has told us, and by the tremendous support and impetus that they gave to the revolutionary elements among the Abolitionists, absolutely prevented the reactionary bourgeoisie—revolutionary later—absolutely prevented the bourgeoisie and the plantocracy from coming to terms as they wanted to do. In 1850 these two made a great attempt at a compromise. What broke that compromise? It was the Fugitive Slave Act. They could prevent everything else for the time being, but they could not prevent the slaves from coming, and the revolutionaries in the North from assisting them. So that we find that here in the history of the United States such is the situation of the masses of the Negro people and their readiness to revolt at the slightest opportunity, that as far back as the Civil War, in relation to the American bourgeoisie, they formed a force which *initiated* and *stimulated* and *acted as a ferment.*

That is point number one.

Point number two. The Civil War takes its course as it is bound to do. Many Negroes and their leaders make an attempt to get incorporated into the Republican Party and to get their cause embraced by the bourgeoisie. And what happens? The bourgeoisie refuses. It doesn't want to have Negroes emancipated. Point number three. As the struggle develops, such is the situation of the Negroes in the United States, that the emancipation of the slaves becomes *an absolute necessity*, politically, organizationally, and from a military point of view.

The Negroes are incorporated into the battle against the South. Not only are they incorporated here, but later they are incorporated also into the military government which smashes down the remnants of resistance in the Southern states. But, when this is done, the Negroes are deserted by the bourgeoisie, *and there falls upon them a very terrible repression.*

That is the course of development in the central episode of American history.

Now if it is so in the Civil War, we have the right to look to see what happened in the War of Independence. It is likely—it is not always certain—but it is *likely* that we shall see there some *anticipations* of the logical development which appeared in the Civil War. They are there. The Negroes begin by demanding their rights. They say if you are asking that the British free you, then we should have our rights, and furthermore, slavery should be abolished. The American bourgeoisie didn't react very well to that. The Negroes insisted—those Negroes who were in the North—insisted that they should be allowed to join the Army of Independence. They were refused.

But later Washington found that it was imperative to have them, and four thousand of them fought among the thirty thousand soldiers of Washington. They gained certain rights after independence was achieved. Then sections of the bourgeoisie who were with them deserted them. And the Negro movement collapsed. We see exactly the same thing but more intensified in the Populist movement. There was a powerful movement of one and one quarter of a million Negroes in the South (the Southern Tenant Farmers' Association). They joined the Populist movement and were in the extreme left wing of this movement, when Populism was discussing whether it should go on with the Democratic Party or make the campaign as a third party. The Negroes voted for the third party and for all the most radical planks in the platform. They fought with the Populist movement. But when Populism was defeated, there fell upon the Negroes between 1896 and about 1910 the desperate, legalized repression and persecution of the Southern states.

Some of us think it is fairly clear that the Garvey movement came and looked to Africa because there was no proletarian movement in the United States to give it a lead, to do for this great eruption of the Negroes what the Civil War and the Populist movement had done for the insurgent Negroes of those days. And now what can we see today? Today the Negroes in the United States are organized as never before. There are more than half a million in the NAACP, and in addition to that, there are all sorts of Negro groups and organizations—the churches in particular—*every single one of which is dominated by the idea that each organization must in some manner or another contribute to the emancipation of the Negroes from capitalist humiliation and from capitalist oppression.* So that the independent Negro movement that we see today and which we see growing before our eyes is nothing strange. It is nothing new. *It is something that has always appeared in the American movement at the first sign of social crisis.*

It represents a climax to the Negro movements that we have seen in the past. From what we have seen in the past, we would expect it to have its head turned towards the labor movement. And not only from a historical point of view but today concrete experience tells us that the masses of the Negro people today look upon the CIO with a respect and consideration that they give to no other social or political force in the country. To anyone who knows the Negro people, who reads their press—and I am not speaking here specially of the Negro workers—if you watch the Negro petty bourgeoisie—reactionary, reformist types as some of them are in all their propaganda, in all their agitation—whenever they are in any difficulties, you can see them leaning toward the labor movement. As for the masses of Negroes, they are increasingly pro-labor every day. So that it is not only Marxist ideas; it is not only a question of Bolshevik-Marxist analysis. It is not only a question of the history of Negroes in the US.

The actual concrete facts before us show us, and anyone who wants to see, this important conclusion, that the Negro movement logically and historically and concretely is headed for the proletariat. That is the road it has always taken in the past, the road to the revolutionary forces. Today the proletariat is that force. And if these ideas that we have traced in American revolutionary crises have shown some power in the past, such is the state of the class struggle today, such the antagonisms between bourgeoisie and proletariat, such, too, the impetus of the Negro *movement toward the revolutionary forces*, which we have traced in the past, is stronger today than ever before. So that we can look upon this Negro movement not only for what it has been and what it has been able to do—we are able to know as Marxists by our own theory and our examination of American history that it is headed for the proletarian movement, that it must go there. There is nowhere else for it to go. And further we can see that if it doesn't go there, the difficulties that the Negroes have suffered in the past when they were deserted by the revolutionary forces, those will be ten, one hundred, ten thousand times as great as in the past. The independent Negro movement, which is boiling and moving, must find its way to the proletariat. If the proletariat is not able to support it, the repression of past times when the revolutionary forces failed the Negroes will be infinitely, I repeat infinitely, more terrible today.

Therefore our consideration of the independent Negro movement does not lessen the significance of the proletarian—the essentially proletarian—leadership. Not at all. It includes it. We are able to see that the mere existence of the CIO, its mere existence, despite the fakery of the labor leadership on the Negro question, as on all other questions, is a protection and a stimulus to the Negroes. We are able to see and I will show in a minute that the Negroes are able by their activity to draw the revolutionary elements and more powerful elements in the proletariat to their side. We are coming to that. But we have to draw and emphasize again and again this important conclusion. If—and we have to take these theoretical questions into consideration—if the proletariat is defeated, if the CIO is destroyed, then there will fall upon the Negro people in the US such a repression, such persecution, comparable to nothing that they have seen in the past.

We have seen in Germany and elsewhere the barbarism that capitalism is capable of in its death agony. The Negro people in the US offer a similar opportunity to the American bourgeoisie. The American bourgeoisie have shown their understanding of the opportunity the Negro question gives them to disrupt and to attempt to corrupt and destroy the labor movement.

But the development of capitalism itself has not only given the independent Negro movement this fundamental and sharp relation with the proletariat. It has created Negro proletarians and placed them as proletarians in what were once the most oppressed and exploited masses. But in auto, steel, and coal, for example, these proletarians have now become the vanguard of the workers' struggle and have brought a substantial number of Negroes to a position of primacy in the struggle against capitalism. The backwardness and humiliation of the Negroes that shoved them into these industries is the very thing which today is bringing them forward, and they are in the very vanguard of the proletarian movement from the very nature of the proletarian struggle itself. Now, how does this complicated interrelationship, the Leninist interrelationship express itself? Henry Ford could write a very good thesis on that if he were so inclined.

The Negroes in the Ford plant were incorporated by Ford: first of all he wanted them for the hard, rough work. I am also informed by the comrades from Detroit he was very anxious to play a paternalistic role with the Negro petty bourgeoisie. He wanted to show them that he was not the person that these people said he was—look! he was giving Negroes opportunities in his plant. Number three, he was able thus to create divisions between whites and Negroes that allowed him to pursue his anti-union, reactionary way.

What has happened within the last few years that is changed? The mass of the Negroes in the River Rouge plant, I am told, are one of the most powerful sections of the Detroit proletariat. They are leaders in the proletarian struggle, not the stooges Ford intended them to be.

Not only that, they act as leaders not only in the labor movement as a whole but in the Negro community. It is what they say that is decisive there. Which is very sad for Henry. And the Negro petty bourgeois have followed the proletariat. They are now going along with the labor movement: they have left Ford too. It is said that he has recognized it at last and that he is not going to employ any more Negroes. He thinks he will do better with women. But they will disappoint him too . . .

Let us not forget that in the Negro people, there sleep and are now awakening passions of a violence exceeding, perhaps, as far as these things can be compared, anything among the tremendous forces that capitalism has created. Anyone who knows them, who knows their history, is able to talk to them intimately, watches them at their own theaters, watches them at their dances, watches them in their churches, reads their press with a discerning eye, must recognize that although their social force may not be able to compare with the social force of a corresponding number of organized workers, the hatred of bourgeois society and the readiness to destroy it when the opportunity should present itself, rests among them to a degree greater than in any other section of the population in the United States.

Sources for Texts

The texts in this volume originally appeared under the pseudonym "J. R. Johnson," except where otherwise indicated. Only "The Revolutionary Answer to the Negro Problem in the United States" (1948) has been reprinted previously.

"Preliminary Notes on the Negro Question" and "Notes Following the Discussion" were originally published in the Socialist Workers Party's *Internal Bulletin*, No. 9 (June 1939), along with the transcripts from James's discussions in Mexico, available in *Leon Trotsky on Black Nationalism and Self-Determination*, ed. George Breitman (New York: Pathfinder Press, 1967).

" 'My Friends': A Fireside Chat on the War," signed "Native Son," was issued as a pamphlet by the Workers Party. It sold for a penny. According to Kent Worcester's *C. L. R. James: A Political Biography* (Albany: State University of New York Press, 1996), the pamphlet was published in June 1940.

"With the Sharecroppers" collects a series of articles published in *Labor Action* during September–October 1941.

"The Economics of Lynching" appeared in James's column "The Negro Question" in *Socialist Appeal*, 10 February 1940.

"The Race Pogroms and the Negro," signed "W. F. Carlton," is from *New International*, July 1943.

"White Workers' Prejudices" appeared in James's column "One-Tenth of a Nation," *Labor Action*, 23 April 1945.

"The Rapid Growth of the NAACP" appeared in *The Militant*, 22 September 1947.

"On *Gone With the Wind*" reprints two texts from *Socialist Appeal*. The first—signed "National Negro Department, Socialist Workers Party"—is from the issue of 30 December 1939. The second, published in the issue of 13 January 1940, appeared in James's regular column "The Negro Question."

"On *Native Son* by Richard Wright" appeared in *Labor Action*, 27 May 1940.

"Public Awareness of the Negro Question," published under the title "Signs of Negro Revolt," is from *Labor Action*, 2 April 1945.

"Joe Louis and Jack Johnson" appeared in *Labor Action*, 1 July 1946.

"The Historical Development of the Negroes in American Society" originally circulated within the Workers Party as a memorandum dated 20 December 1943. It was submitted to the 1944 National Convention of the Workers Party, and first published as "Negroes and the Revolution: Resolution of the Minority" in *The New International*, January 1945.

"The Destiny of the Negro" (1939) appeared as a series in *The Socialist Appeal*, November–December 1939 in connection with a course of lectures by the same title, held at the Marxist School in New York City, sponsored by the Socialist Workers Party.

"Negroes in the Civil War: Their Role in the Second American Revolution" was published in *New International*, December 1943.

"The Two Sides of Abraham Lincoln," is taken from *The Militant*, 14 February 1949. The original text included three paragraphs concerning the 1948 electoral platform of the Socialist Workers Party which have been omitted from this version.

"The 1919 Race Riots in Chicago" appeared in *Socialist Appeal*, 29 August 1939.

"Marcus Garvey" is from *Labor Action*, 24 June 1940.

"The Communist Party's Zigzags on Negro Policy" is an extract from "The SWP Tackles Negro Work," *The Socialist Appeal*, 15 August 1939.

"On *The Negro in the Caribbean* by Eric Williams," published under the pseudonym "W. F. Carlton," appeared as "The West Indies in Review: Recent Developments in the Caribbean Colonies," in *The New International*, June 1943.

"Key Problems in the Study of Negro History" is from *The Militant*, 13 February 1950.

"Lenin on Agriculture and the Negro Question," appeared as James's column "One Tenth of a Nation" in *Labor Action*, 13 January 1947.

"From the Master-Slave Dialectic to Revolt in Capitalist Production" is an extract from "Historical Retrogression or Socialist Revolution," published in *New International*, January 1946.

"Capitalism and the Welfare State" is an extract from "Equality Under the Welfare State," *The Fourth International* (May-June 1950), where it appeared as an unsigned editorial. Both its style and the reference to Marx's "Historical Tendency of Capitalist Accumulation" are characteristically James's.

"The Revolutionary Answer to the Negro Problem in the United States," published under the pseudonym "J. Meyer," appeared in *Fourth International*, December 1948. A few paragraphs concerning internal organizational matters of the Socialist Workers Party have been omitted.

Index